TABLE OF CONTENTS

INTRODUCTION

The 2001 terrorist attacks on the United States have had a substantial and enduring impact on America and its allies. In particular, the United States Department of Defense, which continues to endure the hardships of war in Afghanistan, has fought large-scale major combat operations in Iraq while simultaneously transforming the U.S. military into a counterinsurgency force. After the recent conclusion of the war in Iraq, as the war in Afghanistan draws to a close, and in the context of a struggling U.S. economy, the United States military faces potentially sharp fiscal reductions in the coming months and years. As such, the Department of Defense must make difficult decisions on what capabilities to keep at full strength, which ones to keep at reduced capacity, and which ones to shelve altogether.[1]

The U.S. military's transformation into a counterinsurgency force has come largely at the price of its capability to conduct core competency missions – missions that are essential for major combat operations. As U.S. forces return from today's wars, they will begin another transformation back to their core competencies prompted by a strategy shift toward the Asia-Pacific region,[2] potentially leaving behind many of the lessons from the wars in Iraq and Afghanistan. Many pundits and professionals alike are asking what the correct core competency balance is and how to achieve that balance.

The ensuing debate in this arena is sure to focus on equipment recapitalization requirements, investment in emerging technologies, and force structures to counter

---

[1] U.S. Department of Defense, *Sustaining U.S. Global Leadership: Priorities for 21st Century Defense*, (January 2012), 6.

[2] Ibid., 2.

postulated future threats – especially high-end threats from near-peer competitors.[3] Yet one not-so-obvious capability that is imperative for the U.S. military to maintain is the ability to conduct stability operations as history proves that stability operations are enduring in nature.

The Provincial Reconstruction Team (PRT), a specialized joint civilian-military (CIV-MIL) unit borne out of the wars in Iraq and Afghanistan, is a key asset in the conduct of stability operations. PRTs give the Combatant Commander unique stability operations capabilities, and their worth has been deemed critical in both the Iraq and Afghan theaters of operation.[4] The PRT is unique in that it is an amalgamation of CIV-MIL capabilities and personnel that enable autonomous stability operations in semi-permissive environments to strengthen host nation government capacity and capability, reduce factors which lead to instability, and provide a point of convergence for local, national, and international development initiatives in the area.[5]

Yet even as their contributions have been noted and the Department of Defense (DOD) has issued guidance directing the services to organize, train, and equip for stability operations,[6] the U.S. military has not codified the PRT model; PRTs remain in existence only as *ad hoc* units. In order to institutionally codify the stability operations lessons from the current wars in Iraq and Afghanistan and to ensure that Combatant Commanders are armed with adequate stability operations capabilities for future

---

[3] Ibid., 5.

[4] U.S. House of Representatives, Committee on Armed Services, Subcommittee on Oversight & Investigations, *Agency Stovepipes vs Strategic Agility: Lessons We Need to Learn from Provincial Reconstruction Teams in Iraq and Afghanistan,* (April 2008), 12.

[5] Center for Amry Lessons Learned, *Afghanistan Provincial Reconstruction Team: Observations, Insights, and Lessons,* (February 2011), 2.

[6] U.S. Department of Defense, *DOD Instruction 3000.05: Stability Operations*, (September 16, 2009), 13.

conflicts, the PRT or a variant thereof must become a standing unit within the United States military.

This paper begins its analysis by reviewing and analyzing the current guidance and doctrine on stability operations. It continues by identifying the importance, scope, and relevance of stability operations with the aid of historical accounts as conducted in major combat operations and counterinsurgency campaigns. With a firm doctrinal and historical foundation of stability operations, the paper transitions and conducts a current PRT analysis with an in-depth look at recent U.S. PRT operations in Laghman Province, Afghanistan. The paper concludes with recommendations on how to institutionalize the PRT in the United States military.

This paper limits its scope significantly in the discussion of stability operations in order to maintain an appropriate level of focus within a limited number of pages. To accomplish this, the paper focuses solely on U.S. military Provincial Reconstruction Teams. This is not to detract from the great efforts and successes that coalition partner nations have experienced with their PRTs; coalition PRT efforts merely are beyond the scope of this paper. Similarly, while other U.S. government agencies efforts are integral to PRT operations (namely U.S. Department of State, U.S. Agency for International Development, and U.S. Department of Agriculture), this paper narrows its interagency focus to that which occurs within a U.S. PRT.

The scope is also limited to an in-depth study of one U.S. PRT located in Laghman Province. As one would expect with *ad hoc* units operating in a diverse and mature theater of operations, each U.S. PRT in Afghanistan is unique in its organization and approach to the problems within its area of operations. An exhaustive study of each

U.S. PRT would be required should the Services decide to institutionalize PRTs into standing units, but such a wide level of analysis is beyond the scope of this study.

Lastly, this paper is limited to open source, unclassified information. Certainly some fidelity is lost with the exclusion of classified material, especially where the paper turns its focus on PRT operations in Afghanistan. However, this does not detract from the greater argument that the paper poses.

CHAPTER 1: GUIDANCE AND DOCTRINE

Guidance and doctrine as they apply to U.S. Provincial Reconstruction Teams are somewhat limited. PRTs as they are known today are a relatively new concept with somewhat shallow roots in the Iraqi and Afghan theaters of operation. However, the stability operations mission is longstanding, and its importance is undisputed.[1] This chapter reviews the current guidance from the strategic to the tactical levels as the beginning of an assessment of the relationship between guidance and how the US military is organized, trained, and equipped to conduct enduring stability operations missions.

Department of Defense (DOD) guidance for stability operations was initially codified in Department of Defense Directive 3000.05 (DODD 3000.05), "Military Support for Stability, Security, Transition, and Reconstruction (SSTR) Operations."[2] Dated November 28, 2005, this document highlights the recent emphasis on stability operations and the relative infancy of DOD-level stability operations guidance. Current department level guidance is presented in Department of Defense Instruction (DODI) 3000.05, September 16, 2009 and supersedes the aforementioned directive.[3] This document largely defines the strategic policy from which PRT operations are derived and identifies both the DOD's and the services' roles in conducting stability operations.

---

[1] U.S. Department of Defense, *DoD Instruction 3000.05*, 5.

[2] U.S. Department of Defense, *DoD Directive 3000.05: Stability Operations*, (November 28, 2005).

[3] U.S. Department of Defense, *DoD Instruction 3000.05*, 1.

U.S. Military Joint doctrine is codified in the Joint Staff's Joint Publication 3-07, *Stability Operations*, dated 29 September 2011.[4] This publication provides comprehensive doctrine on conducting stability operations in the larger context of full spectrum operations, identifies essential tasks, outlines planning principles, and describes transitional military authority and security sector reform operations.[5] Each of these documents is reviewed in depth in the following pages.[6]

Department of Defense Instruction 3000.05

The importance of Department of Defense Instruction (DODI) 3000.05 is paramount to the discussion of how United States military organizes, trains, and equips to conduct stability operations. This instruction dominates the high-level stability operations landscape as it dictates, from a national level, that the conduct of stability operations is an enduring mission for the Department of Defense and that the services will appropriately prepare to conduct this mission set.

The instruction explicitly defines stability operations "as an overarching term encompassing various military missions, tasks, and activities conducted outside the United States in coordination with other instruments of national power to maintain or reestablish a safe and secure environment, provide essential governmental services,

---

[4] U.S. Joint Chiefs of Staff, *Stability Operations*, Joint Pubilcation 3-07 (Washington DC: Joint Chiefs of Staff, 29 September 2011).

[5] Ibid., vii. For an example of service-specific stability operations doctrine, see U.S. Army Field Manual 3-07, *Stability Operations*, dated October 2008.

[6] Specific to PRT operations, the aforementioned higher level publications are complimented by "Afghanistan Provincial Reconstruction Team: Observations, Insights, and Lessons," a Center for Army Lessons Learned (CALL) publication that identifies PRT best practices, pitfalls to avoid, and useful tactics, techniques, and procedures. While this document is neither doctrine nor guidance, it will be thoroughly examined in Chapter 3. Center for Army Lessons Learned, *Afghanistan Provincial Reconstruction Team*, (February 2011).

emergency infrastructure reconstruction, and humanitarian relief."[7] Further, it states that "stability operations are a core U.S. military mission that the Department of Defense shall be prepared to conduct with proficiency equivalent to combat operations."[8]

In the conduct of this mission set, the instruction identifies three capacities in which the Department of Defense must prepare for stability operations. First, the department must be prepared to carry out stability operations across the spectrum of conflict in short, medium, and long duration engagements. Second, it must support stability operations that are conducted by other U.S. Government departments or agencies, foreign governments, or other entities as directed by the Department of Defense. Third, it must be prepared to "lead stability operations activities to establish civil security and civil control, restore essential services, repair and protect critical infrastructure, and deliver humanitarian assistance until such time as it is feasible to transition lead responsibility to other U.S. Government agencies, foreign government and security forces, or international governmental organizations."[9]

The instruction states that DOD capabilities must be interoperable and complimentary with other U.S. and foreign government efforts, and it specifies that the DOD will be prepared to carry out the following mission sets:[10]

- Establish civil security and civil control.
- Restore or provide essential services.
- Repair critical infrastructure.
- Provide humanitarian assistance.

---

[7] U.S. Department of Defense, *DoD Instruction 3000.05*, 1.

[8] Ibid.

[9] Ibid.

[10] Ibid.

The instruction consistently highlights the importance of a whole of government approach in the conduct of stability operations. Specifically regarding Department of Defense assistance to other agencies in the conduct of stability operations, the instructions states that the DOD will assist other agencies with the following mission sets:[11]

- Disarming, demobilizing, and reintegrating former belligerents into civil society.
- Rehabilitating former belligerents and units into legitimate security forces.
- Strengthening governance and the rule of law.
- Fostering economic stability and development.

Perhaps most importantly, the instruction states that "the DOD Components shall explicitly address and integrate stability operations-related concepts and capabilities across doctrine, organization, training, materiel, leadership and education, personnel, facilities, and applicable exercises, strategies, and plans."[12]

This overarching guidance is complemented by instructions to guide efforts among government agencies, including policy formulation, interagency coordination and integration, and strategy and plan preparation. The instruction specifies that the Department of Defense will

> ...develop policies to recruit, select, and assign civilian DOD personnel with relevant skills for service in stability operations assignments, ...develop policies and programs to maintain the appropriate levels of civilian and military language and cultural understanding, and... establish policy and procedures to be used by the DOD Components to determine the total force requirements (i.e. military, DOD civilian, and contractor requirements) necessary for conducting stability operations.[13]

---

[11] Ibid., 3.

[12] Ibid.

[13] Ibid., 10.

Regarding the U.S. military services, it instructs the service secretaries to "develop and maintain scalable capabilities and capacities to establish civil security and civil control, restore essential services, repair critical infrastructure, and provide humanitarian relief across the range of military activities" and to "maintain a civilian and military workforce capable of sustained contributions to civil-military teams conducting stability operations activities."[14] In the conduct of these tasks, it identifies the requirements to establish relevant doctrine, mission-essential tasks and capabilities, readiness requirements, training programs, force availability, and predeployment training venues for stability operations forces.[15]

The significance of DODI 3000.05 as relating to Provincial Reconstruction Teams is threefold. First, it establishes definitive guidance that stability operations are a core capability of the United States military and that the services must organize, train, and equip to that end. Second, the instruction establishes the importance of a whole of government approach in the conduct of stability operations. Third, it is important to note that the instruction directs the services to recruit and maintain a cadre of personnel with special capabilities in the conduct of stability operations. Each of these points has direct implications for Provincial Reconstruction Teams, as each plays a role in PRT organization and operations. These points are further discussed in Chapter 3 as the paper analyzes an Afghanistan-based U.S. PRT.

---

[14] Ibid., 10.

[15] Ibid., 13.

Joint Publication 3-07, *Stability Operations*

If one considers DODI 3000.05 as strategic-level guidance for stability operations wherein U.S. government ends and means are established, Joint Publication 3-07 (JP 3-07) should be considered operational level guidance for stability operations. In this capacity, JP 3-07 takes the strategic guidance from DODI 3000.05, establishes the means by which stability operations are conducted, and adds a level of fidelity that guides the tactical conduct of stability operations.

Nature of Stability Operations

"The primary military contribution to stabilization is to protect and defend the population, facilitating the personal security of the people and, thus, creating a platform for political, economic, and human security."[16] With this quote defining DOD's role in the conduct of stability operations, one would expect this role to neatly nest with the aforementioned definition of stability operations from DODI 3000.05.[17] In the offense, defense, stability operations continuum of military operations, JP-3-07 states that "…stability operations is a core U.S. military mission that the Armed Forces are prepared to conduct with proficiency equivalent to combat operations," succinctly highlighting the importance of the conduct of stability operations to the joint force.[18] Although all joint forces conduct stability operations, because stability operations are conducted on land, "joint land forces (to include SOF [special operations forces]) will normally provide the majority of the force required supported by joint air, maritime, and space forces."[19]

---

[16] Joint Chiefs of Staff, *Stability Operations,* I-2.

[17] JP 3-07's definition of stability operations is taken verbatim from DODI 3000.05.

[18] Ibid.

[19] Ibid., II-14.

JP 3-07 broadly defines stability operations in terms of three major groupings of effort: initial response activities, transformational activities, and sustainment activities.[20] Initial response activities focus on rapidly establishing security in the wake of a significant event such as a natural disaster or combat operations. These activities are essential to limit human suffering while simultaneously enabling conditions in the operational environment that allow for transformational and sustaining activities.[21]

Transformational activities are those that expand the circle of security allowed by initial response activities. They offer a broad range of security, reconstruction, and capacity building activities that build host nation capacity and capability across multiple lines of effort.[22]

Sustainment efforts are those that enable host nation entities to continue operations without external support. These efforts are marked by long-term capacity-building, reconstruction, and development efforts that create conditions to enable long-term sustainable development in the area.[23] The conceptual synchronization of initial response, transformational, and sustainment activities create a continuum of stability operations efforts that can be visualized over time; this continuum is depicted in Figure 1.

---

[20] Ibid., I-3.

[21] Ibid., I-4.

[22] Ibid.

[23] Ibid.

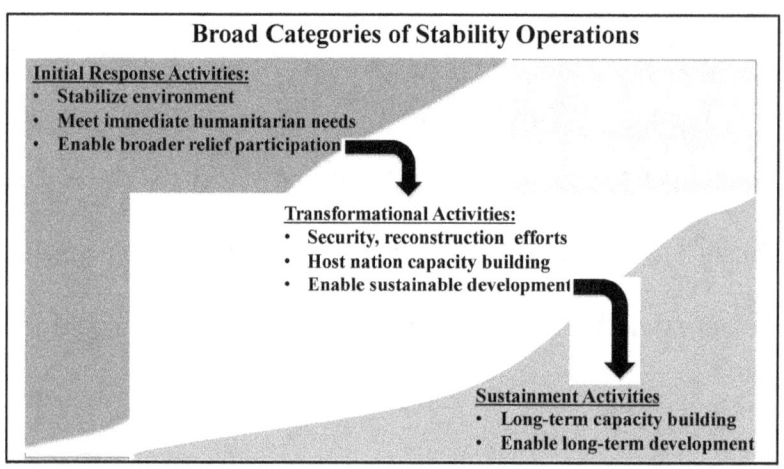

Figure 1: Broad Categories of Stability Operations[24]

Figure 1 is instructive in that it conceptually portrays the different categories of stability

operations and how they relate to each other as functions of effort and time. Early efforts

in a stability operation are almost entirely initial response activities (depicted in orange),

which gradually give way to transformational activities (depicted in yellow), which

gradually give way to sustainment activities (depicted in blue). This interrelation enables

the growth and sustainment of host nation capabilities and capacities that ultimately

promise the redeployment of U.S. stability operations forces in conjunction with the

transfer of authority to host nation entities. While the different categories in actuality are

perhaps more of a continuum than depicted in the figure, different phases of stability

operations are marked by different levels of effort within these categories, underscoring

the importance of design and planning efforts for stability operations, both of which are

discussed in the following pages.

---

[24] Ibid.

Stability Operations Design and Planning

Stability operations are one of a triumvirate of joint operations, the other two being offense and defense. Offensive, defensive, and stability operations work in concert with each other to achieve joint force objectives in the operational environment.[25] As the three are intrinsically linked, so must their planning efforts be. "The balance and simultaneity in execution of offense, defense, and stability operations within each phase of a joint operation demands a similar balance and simultaneity in planning efforts."[26]

Stability operations planning, from the perspective of a planning process, mirrors the planning of any other military operation as described in Joint Publication 5-0, *Joint Operation Planning*.[27] Yet stability operations have four employment phases that are unique. These phases are illustrated in Figure 2 and described below.

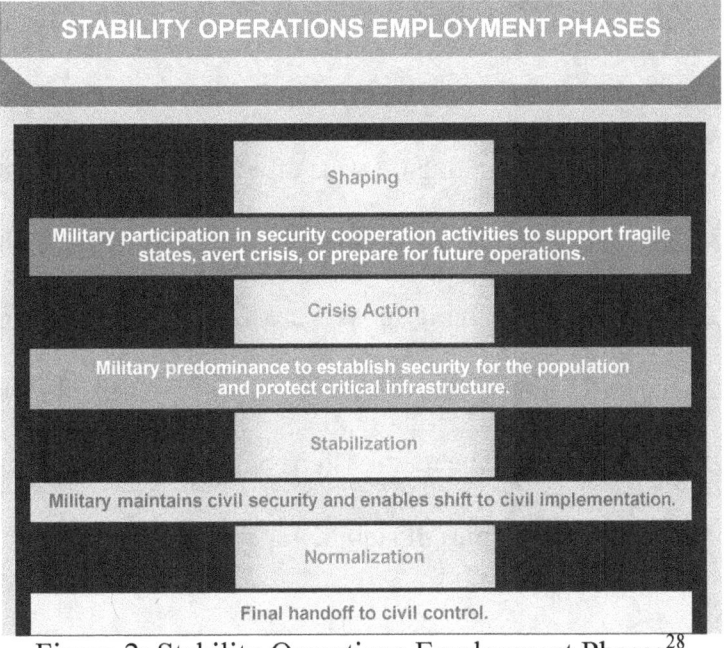

Figure 2: Stability Operations Employment Phases[28]

---

[25] Ibid., II-1.

[26] Ibid.

[27] Ibid., II-2.

[28] Ibid., II-11.

As one analyzes Figure 2, it becomes evident that in the conduct of stability operations, the military is employed only as a nonpermanent force; when civil authorities are able to care for and control the population, final handoff to civil control occurs. This concept highlights a key tenet of planning stability operations, as close and constant interaction with civil entities is required for the ultimate success of the mission.[29]

As described by Joint Publication 5-0, *Joint Operation Planning*, portions of joint operations are phased in time and space that logically link together to form the entire campaign or operation; the notional operation plan phases are Shape, Deter, Seize Initiative, Dominate, Stabilize, and Enable Civil Authority.[30] As stability operations are incorporated into a joint operation plan, the stability operations employment phases are woven into the operational phasing model.[31] During each phase, stability operations are arranged in time and space to work synergistically with offensive and defense operations to achieve the joint force commander's objectives. During the different phases, stability operations will ebb and flow, depending on what effects are required in the battle space. Conceptually speaking, although stability operations can occur in each phase, the shape, deter, stabilize, and enable civil authority phases are marked by large stability operations efforts, while the seize the initiative and dominate phases are marked by large offense and defense operations efforts.[32] The relationships between phases are further discussed in Chapter 2 using historical examples of stability operations.

---

[29] Ibid., I-20.

[30] U.S. Joint Chiefs of Staff, *Joint Operation Planning*, Joint Pubilcation 5-0, (Washington DC: Joint Chiefs of Staff, 11 August 2011).

[31] U.S. Joint Chiefs of Staff, *Stability Operations*, II-12.

[32] Ibid., II-15.

Stability Operations Functions

Within the stability operations phases, there are five stability operations functions

that comprise the larger stability operations mission set. These functions are: [33]

- Security
- Humanitarian assistance
- Economic stabilization and infrastructure
- Rule of law
- Governance and participation

Each of these functions is evident in historical stability operations (discussed in Chapter

2), is intrinsically linked to PRT operations (discussed in Chapter 3), and is discussed in

detail in the following pages.

Security

> *And security is not an end in itself. Key to overall success here is the conduct of orchestrated actions across the three lines of operations - security, governance and reconstruction. Improved security conditions will allow the Afghan government, supported by the international community, to search [sic] governance and reconstruction initiatives. This will be mutually beneficial as there is neither reconstruction nor good governance without security and no lasting security without reconstruction and good governance.* [34]

Security is not an end unto itself, and similarly the establishment of security does

not constitute a stability operation. [35] Rather, the ultimate goal of security in the conduct

of stability operations is to create a level of security that enables the conduct of the other

stability operations functions. To this end, stability operations forces must conduct an

---

[33] Ibid., III-2.

[34] Major General Kasdorf, Chief of Staff, International Security Assistance Force teleconference, (1 October 2007), http://www.nato.int/isaf/docu/speech/2007/sp071011a.html (accessed February 25, 2012).

[35] U.S. Joint Chiefs of Staff, *Stability Operations*, III-4.

evaluation of the security in the operational environment (OE) and then tailor security operations to the environment.[36]

The analysis of the security situation is not limited strictly to the conduct of the security mission set. While it does establish a level of required security and the actions that will be required to establish or re-establish security, the analysis leads to a broader understanding of the OE and links directly to the other mission sets within stability operations.[37] In other words, security operations involve the direct application of force to create a secure environment which, in turn, enable other operations in the OE to take place.[38] Thus, while security is not an end to itself, it is a necessary prerequisite for the accomplishment of further stability operations functions.[39]

Humanitarian Assistance

The provision of humanitarian assistance (HA) includes actions taken that assist providing the basic needs of the population, e.g. water, food, shelter, sanitation, and health services, that ultimately return normalcy to the population's way of life.[40]

Military contributions in the conduct of HA include the transportation and delivery of relief supplies; the provision for medical, surgical, dental and veterinary care; the construction of rudimentary surface transportation systems and public facilities; and

---

[36] Ibid., III-5. The OE's security situation can broadly be divided into three subsets: Hostile, where the emphasis is to establish security, usually sector by sector; Uncertain, where the emphasis is to hold and improve the current level of security; and Permissive, where the emphasis is to provide force protection to friendly forces.

[37] Ibid., III-7.

[38] Ibid., III-5, 11.

[39] Ibid. Joint forces may be required to perform Security Sector Reform (SSR) as part of stability operations. SSR includes policies, plans, programs, and activities to provide safety, security, and justice to the population. For further detail, refer to JP 3-07, Appendix C, "Security Sector Reform".

[40] Ibid., III-18.

the provision for basic water and sanitation facilities.[41] Military forces may also be required to conduct missions to support dislocated civilians, emergency food assistance/food security, shelter construction, and health and education support.[42] It is important to consider that the military effort in the conduct of HA is usually in a supporting role to civilian agencies. As such, military forces generally provide "stop-gap" measures in the initial stages of disaster relief until HA missions can be handed over to the host nation, international, or other U.S. Government agency.[43]

Economic Stabilization and Infrastructure

The goal of economic stabilization and infrastructure is to provide a sustainable economic system that allows the opportunity for individuals to prosper in a stable economic system that is governed by law.[44] Building in concert with the stabilizing effects of security and humanitarian assistance, economic stabilization and infrastructure addresses causal economic drivers of instability while enabling an environment that fosters political solutions.[45] Actions taken by stability operations forces are not small undertakings, often requiring significant force presence in both size and duration, and include:

> …[R]estoring employment opportunities, initiating market reform, mobilizing
> domestic and foreign investment, supervising monetary reform, and rebuilding
> public structures. Infrastructure restoration consists of the reconstitution of
> power, transportation, communications, health and sanitation, fire fighting,

---

[41] Ibid., III-20. For further detail, refer to JP 3-29, *Foreign Humanitarian Assistance*, JP 3-57, *Civil-Military Operations*, and JP 3-22, *Foreign Internal Defense*.

[42] Ibid., III-23-26. A recent U.S. force example of these activities is tsunami relief in Indonesia in 2004-5.

[43] Ibid., III-26.

[44] Ibid., III-27.

[45] Ibid.

education, mortuary services, and environmental control. This includes restoring the functioning of economic production and distribution.[46]

Although economic stabilization and infrastructure roles are "inherently civilian undertakings," military presence and efforts are typically critical to the mission set, especially when the security conditions preclude civilian agency freedom of movement.[47] In such a case, "economic stabilization tasks should normally be conducted by a PRT or some other interagency field-based team" in order to assemble a combined effort to address advancement of the host nation's governance and economic capabilities and capacities.[48]

Although the military contribution to economic stabilization and infrastructure is similar to that associated with humanitarian assistance (i.e., primarily in a supporting role as a "stop-gap" measure), military forces may be called upon to generate employment, establish monetary systems, foster fiscal policy and governance, and develop critical infrastructure.[49] One method that military units employ to provide these functions is with Quick Impact Projects (QIPs). QIPs strive to provide visible, short-term provisions to the population in order to establish and reinforce the governance capability and perception of the host nation governance.[50]

> Where PRTs or other interagency field-based teams (e.g., FACTs [Field Advance Civilian Team]) exist, much of this activity will be funded, planned, and implemented by development agencies coordinated through the PRT or

---

[46] Ibid.

[47] Ibid.

[48] Ibid., III-28. For a detailed discussion on economic stabilization and infrastructure, see U.S. Joint Forces Command Joint Force Commander's Handbook, *Military Support to Economic Normalization*.

[49] Ibid., III-31, 32. Examples of critical infrastructure cited in JP 3-07 include water and sanitation facilities, agriculture value chains, transportation networks, information and communications technology networks, energy systems, and production enterprise facilities.

[50] Ibid., III-35.

interagency team. In these circumstances, development and security activities will need to be mutually reinforcing within a civil-military integrated plan.[51]

The PRT's implementation of QIPs, use of Commander's Emergency Response Program funding, and coordination with development agencies is discussed in chapter 3.

Rule of Law

Rule of law functions establish accountability, under law, for the conduct of day to day activities within the society. Rule of law is a system of systems that implements "just legal frameworks, public order, accountability to the law, access to justice, and a culture of lawfulness... to ensure all individuals and institutions, public and private, and the state itself are held accountable to the law."[52] Rule of law enables the legitimate power of the government by ensuring the following:[53]

- The state has a monopoly on the use of force in the resolution of disputes.
- Individuals are secure in their persons and property.
- The state is bound by law and does not act arbitrarily.
- Laws can be readily determined; allow the population to plan its affairs.
- Individuals have access to an effective and impartial justice system.
- The state protects basic human rights and fundamental freedoms.
- Individuals understand and respect judicial institutions and develop a belief in their equity and fairness that guides the conduct of the daily lives.

Depending upon the nature of the operational environment, the military's contribution to the rule of law mission set may differ significantly. A broad spectrum of professionals, such as "judges, prosecutors, court administrators, defense lawyers, corrections personnel, law enforcement, and investigators" may be required to establish a rule of law system; however, if joint forces are conducting stability operations in a failed

---

[51] Ibid.

[52] Ibid., III-41.

[53] Ibid. For a detailed discusstion on rule of law, see U.S. Joint Forces Command's Joint Force Commander's Handbook: *Military Support to Rule of Law and Security Sector Reform.*

state these functions may require staffing by military personnel.[54] In such an instance, military members may be required to establish an interim criminal justice system, create personal property dispute resolution mechanisms, and establish war crimes tribunals and truth commissions.[55]

Governance and Participation

Governance and participation provides the mechanisms that effectively connect the government with the population. Effective governance provides services for the population, holds government officials accountable, and provides mechanisms for the lawful and nonviolent involvement of individuals and political parties in government systems.[56]

> Stable governance provides a foundation on which rule of law and economic activity can thrive and become drivers of security and stability. Support to effective governance involves establishing rules and procedures for political decision making, strengthening public sector management and administrative institutions and practices, providing public services in an effective and transparent manner, and providing civil administration that supports lawful economic activity and enterprise.[57]

Military contributions to governance and participation may be very limited, such as election security, or very involved, such as establishing a temporary military government in a failed state. Other military missions may include supporting the national

---

[54] Ibid., III-46.

[55] Ibid., III-46. Establishing an interim criminal justice system includes efforts with police forces, legal frameworks, judicial systems, and penal systems.

[56] Ibid., III-47.

[57] Ibid., III-48. For a detailed discussion on governance and participation, see U.S. Joint Forces Command's Joint Force Commander's Handbook, *Military Support to Governance, Elections, and Media.*

constitution process, supporting transitional governance, supporting local governance, supporting anticorruption initiatives, and supporting elections.[58]

Governance and participation is inherently linked to the other functions of stability operations, and as one begins to grasp the continuum of stability operations functions, it becomes apparent that for stability operations to be successful, especially in weak or failed states, military units must adopt a comprehensive, integrated approach in order to achieve mission success.

Guidance and Doctrine Summary

In the context of current U.S. military stability operations guidance and doctrine evolution, one cannot help but be reassured that DOD is working to provide current, relevant information to the Joint Force. Indeed, both DOD and the services have certainly adapted to the operational demands posed by ongoing stability operations both operationally and doctrinally.

However, without lasting changes to the military's organizational structure at the tactical level, these changes have little chance of weathering the inevitable downsizing that the military will experience in the post-Operation Enduring Freedom/Operation Iraqi Freedom (OEF/OIF) era. Historical examples of previous stability operation experiences highlight the enduring nature of stability operations and the necessity to capture – in a lasting manner – the stability operations lessons that our military institution has recently identified.

Department of Defense Instruction 3000.05 and JP 3-07 are explicit in their definition of and requirement for the conduct of stability operations. There are several

---

[58] Ibid., III-49-51. For a detailed discusson on military governance, refer to JP 3-07, *Stability Operations*, Annex D, "Transitional Military Authority."

instructive points that one can glean from its content. First, stability operations are conducted outside the United States, separating them from defense support to civil authority mission set. Moreover, this requirement drives the need for Joint Force deployment requirements to conduct stability operations. Second, stability operations are conducted with other instruments of national and international power, meaning that they are both inherently joint and integrated with interagency partners in the conduct of the mission. Third, stability operations include Security, Humanitarian Assistance, Economic Stabilization and Infrastructure, Rule of Law, and Governance and Participation functions. These functions are stated requirements for the conduct of stability operations, and each of them forms a portion of the foundation of the PRT.

Both documents are also conclusive in their requirements both for the conduct of stability operations and for the sustained requirement of stability operations-capable forces. DODI 3000.05's description of "scalable capabilities and capacities" of a workforce "capable of sustained contributions to civil-military teams conducting stability operations activities"[59] coupled with JP 3-07's specific references to the use of PRTs in the conduct of stability operations certainly appears to lead the services toward sustaining the current PRT model. Although DODI 3000.05 is not restrictive as to the unit type that is required to conduct stability operations, it does not say that the stability operations workforce must be dedicated only to the stability operations mission. In other words, the DODI leads the military to determine if other forces (e.g., infantry or special operations forces units augmented with specialized civilian and military personnel) are sufficient for the conduct of stability operations.

---

[59] DODI 3000.05, 13.

CHAPTER 2: HISTORICAL EXAMPLES OF STABILITY OPERATIONS

History provides ample examples of forces conducting stability operations. Even if one were to limit the scope of research to American case studies, examples include the American Civil War, the two World Wars, the Korean War, the Vietnam War, the Iraq War, and the current war in Afghanistan, not to mention numerous humanitarian assistance/disaster relief stability operations missions. While each of these conflicts/events have their own nuances where stability operations is concerned, they all reveal a narrative that underscores the importance of stability operations, how they are employed in time and space under the greater context of a campaign plan, and how they link with other government or non-government organizations in the battle space. Two examples are explored in this chapter. The first is post-WWII Japan and highlights the relationship of stability operations to major combat operations; the second is the Philippine War and highlights the relationship of stability operations to counterinsurgency operations.

Major Combat Operations: Post-World War II Japan

WWII demonstrated with unprecedented clarity the close interconnection between military and civilian affairs; nowhere was this connection more evident than in military government. Yet no task undertaken by the Army produced more misunderstanding at high levels of Government. Orderly civil administration must be maintained in support of military operations in liberated and occupied territories.[1]

Post World War II Japan was marked largely by devastation. 65 percent of Tokyo was destroyed; Nagasaki and Hiroshima lay in ruins; nine million Japanese were

---

[1] Henry L. Stimson and McGeorge Bundy, *On Active Service in Peace and War*, (New York: Harper & Brothers, 1947), 553.

homeless; and the country was largely helpless to support its population as a result of the massively drained resources by 13 years of war.[2] Although the United States sought and achieved the end of the war on the terms of unconditional surrender, it realized the strategic importance of disarming Japan and maintaining Japan's support in a potential future conflict with the Union of Soviet Socialist Republics.[3] The American task was clear; it would have to engage in large-scale stability operations (which was referred to as "nation-building" at the time) in post-war Japan, and as the Supreme Commander of Allied Powers in charge of the operation, the responsibility of the task would lie largely with General Douglas MacArthur.

At the conclusion of the war, the United States outlined a set of objectives as part of the Potsdam Declaration. These included the removal of militarist leadership and the demilitarization of the county; limiting Japanese sovereignty to the islands of Honshu, Hokkaido, Kyushu, and Shikoku (return of wartime land gains); bringing justice to war criminals; strengthening of democratic principles; and economic/industrial demilitarization.[4] To meet these objectives the declaration stated that occupational forces would be allowed until the objectives were met.

The Potsdam Declaration was the end result of years of planning for the end of the war with Japan. Planning in the State Department began in 1943 with the establishment of the Interdivisional Areas Committee on the Far East and was joined by

[2] Katherine Rogers, "The Interagency Process in Reconstruction of Post-World War II Japan," in *The Interagency Counterinsurgency Warfare: Stability, Security, Transition, and Reconstruction Roles* (Carlisle, PA: Strategic Studies Institute, 2007), http://www.isn.ethz.ch/isn/Digital-Library/Publications/Detail/?ots591=cab359a3-9328-19cc-a1d2-8023e646b22c&lng=en&id=48234 (accessed 4 January 2012), 171-207, passage from 172.

[3] Ibid., 173.

[4] Japan Government, "Potsdam Declaration," National Diet Library, http://www.ndl.go.jp/constitution/e/etc/c06.html (accessed 4 January 2012).

efforts from the Navy and War Departments in 1944.[5] In December 1944 the Secretaries

of State, War, and Navy agreed to appoint a committee to coordinate post-war matters

that were common to all of the departments, ultimately resulting in the formulation of the

State-War-Navy Coordinating Committee (SWNCC).[6]

> Within SWNCC, policy formulation was delegated downward, with the main
> responsibility centered at the assistant secretary level. These key assistant
> secretaries further delegated their authority downward and outward (horizontally),
> incorporating all available experts within and outside government. As a result,
> the effort became a true "whole-of-government" (WOG) effort, rather than a
> simpler division of authority in an all-of-government effort, such as we currently
> have. The result was that there was a premium on policy consensus which
> allowed organizations and individuals to cooperate as equals and have
> "ownership" of policies.[7]

Interestingly, the vast majority of the reconstruction effort was carried out by the

War Department via General MacArthur's staffs and military forces in theater.[8] In a

memo drafted by Secretary of State James Byrnes and later forwarded and approved by

President Truman, the State Department would take the lead on policy formulation, to

include chairing the SWNCC, while the War Department led all execution and

administration efforts.[9] "In part due to this memo, the reconstruction of Japan remained

a military mission for all 7 years of the occupation, rather than transitioning to civil

authorities."[10]

---

[5] Rogers, "The Interagency Process in Reconstruction of Post-World War II Japan," 174.

[6] Ibid.

[7] Peter F. Schaefer and P. Clayton Schaefer, "Planning for Reconstruction and Transformation of Japan after World War II," in *Stability Operations and State Building,* (Strategic Studies Institute, 2008), http://www.isn.ethz.ch/isn/Digital-Library/Publications/Detail/?ots591=cab359a3-9328-19cc-a1d2-8023e646b22c&lng=en&id=92327 (accessed January 4, 2012), 69-88, passage from 70.

[8] Ibid., 178.

[9] Ibid.

[10] Ibid. This is not to say that the mission was entirely military; the same memo also recommended support to the War Department with "suitable civilian personnel to complete the

As the executor of such a grand undertaking, General MacArthur found himself dual-hatted as the Supreme Commander of Allied Powers (SCAP) and as the commander of the Army's Far East Command (FEC). In an attempt to build staff efficiencies, General MacArthur divided his staff along two functional lines: occupation and reconstruction. Using this construct he assigned occupation duties to the FEC General Headquarters (GHQ) and assigned reconstruction duties to the SCAP GHQ.[11] As such, an interesting and ingenious organizational structure emerged.

> Both headquarters would be under MacArthur and the same Chief of Staff, but would operate more or less independently of one another. FEC GHQ would bear responsibility for the bulk of military occupation and security responsibilities. On the other side, SCAP GHQ would manage the many processes associated with nation-building [stability operations]. The majority of the regular Army worked in FEC GHQ, while SCAP GHQ consisted mostly of reserve officers with a civilian perspective. This organizational structure largely removed the career military from the process of democratization, and eased the inherent tension between the necessary autocracy of military culture and the requirements of a budding democracy.[12]

To put General MacArthur's staff organization into current terms, he roughly divided his headquarters between the Security stability operations function for FEC GHQ (military occupation and security responsibilities) and the Humanitarian Assistance, Economic Stabilization and Infrastructure, Rule of Law, and Governance and Participation functions for SCAP GHQ (stability operations).

As an instrument of discussing the unique headquarters organization implemented by General MacArthur, this paper discusses the accomplishment of Strengthening Democracy and Economic Demilitarization set out by the Potsdam Declaration in the

---

necessary field staff to discharge the War Department responsibility for government in the Occupied Areas by assignment of their existing personnel and facilities, by assistance in recruiting specially qualified persons, and in all other practibale action."

[11] Ibid., 178-9.

[12] Ibid., 179.

following pages. While military disarmament, the return of occupied territories, and bringing justice to war criminals certainly played key roles in U.S. efforts in postwar Japan, strengthening democracy and economic demilitarization provide poignant lessons in the conduct of stability operations following major combat operations.

Strengthening Democracy

Early in 1946, virtually on the spur of the moment, General MacArthur initiated what he later called "probably the single most important accomplishment of the occupation" – nothing less than the replacing of the Meiji Constitution of 1890 with a new national charter.[13]

The postwar evolution of Japanese government was directed – albeit loosely – by the Potsdam Declaration via three sections. Section 6 stated, "There must be eliminated for all time the authority and influence of those who have deceived and misled the people of Japan into embarking on world conquest."[14] Section 10 stated that "the Japanese government shall remove all obstacles to the revival and strengthening of democratic tendencies among the Japanese people. Freedom of speech, of religion, and of thought, as well as respect for fundamental human rights, shall be established."[15] Further, Section 12 stated that "the occupying forces of the Allies shall be withdrawn from Japan as soon as these objectives have been accomplished and there has been established in accordance with the freely expressed will of the Japanese people a peacefully inclined and responsible government."[16]

---

[13] John W. Dower, *Embracing Defeat: Japan in the Wake of World War II*, (New York: W.W. Norton & Company, 2000), 346.

[14] Government Section, General Headquarters, Supreme Commander for the Allied Powers, *Political Reorientation of Japan: September 1945 to September 1948*, (Washington DC: U.S. Government Printing Office, 1949), I:89-90, as quoted in Dower, 347.

[15] Ibid.

[16] Ibid.

The onset of democratic reform of the Japanese government was spurred by a top-secret cable from policy makers in Washington to General MacArthur. This memo called "for changes in the 'governmental system' to create genuinely representative suffrage, popular control over the executive branch, a strengthened elective legislature, guarantees of fundamental civil rights, and greater local autonomy."[17] Initial efforts by General MacArthur and his staffs to affect Japanese government changes in order to meet the requirements set forth by the Potsdam Proclamation and guidance from Washington were troubled. It rapidly became clear that the members of the Japanese government had very little incentive to meet these requirements, the imperial family's efforts, while concerted, would not meet with Washington's scope or intent of change, and the privileged men from the Meiji period simply did not comprehend the gravity of the situation.[18]

> …[H]ere was the nub of the problem: what really made democratization possible was neither the old constitution nor the "moderate" old civilian elites, but the new reformist overlords, the alien Americans; and in their view, there were no constitutional protections to prevent the system from clamping shut again once they left town. This was what the Japanese conservatives utterly failed to comprehend.[19]

Thus in February 1946 General MacArthur, convinced that democratic reform of the Japanese government would have to be driven from the SCAP GHQ, assembled a planning team within the Government Section of SCAP. General MacArthur charged the team with drafting a new Constitution for Japan; a task that was to be completed between the 4th and 12th of February, 1946.[20] The Government Section team, comprised of 16 officers and eight civilians, four of whom were women, did not include any professional

---

[17] Ibid., 348.

[18] Ibid., 348-52.

[19] Ibid., 352.

[20] Ibid., 360.

military individuals yet included four lawyers, a former Congressman, professors of social science and business, and a foreign service officer.[21] This unique mix of personnel allowed the team to succeed in producing a draft Constitution in just a week; General MacArthur approved the document on the 11th of February 1946.

In the ensuing weeks, SCAP coordinated with the Japanese Emperor and his staff to translate and "Japanize" the new Constitution, release it to the Japanese people, and deliver it to the Diet (Japanese Parliament) for revision, approval, and implementation. On the 3rd of May 1947, the newly ratified Japanese Constitution became the law of the land in Japan.

Economic Demilitarization

In the wake of defeat, Japan's entire productive structure had come to a standstill "as if a big wheel had stopped turning." The challenge was to get this wheel moving again by mobilizing big capital in optimally rational ways.[22]

The post-war Japanese economy could be described as a catastrophic disaster. Few Japanese government officials had put any real thought into what a post-war economic system would look like, much less how to establish and run such a system.[23] Added to this, as the government churned out reams of freshly printed currency to provide severance pay to millions of demilitarized soldiers and laid-off workers, plummeting the economic system, and marking "the beginning of the ravenous inflation that ultimately drained the economy."[24]

---

[21] Ibid., 364-5.

[22] Ibid., 538-9.

[23] Ibid.

[24] Ibid., 531.

SCAP began the arduous task of transforming the Japanese economy by targeting the *zaibatsu*, a "large family-controlled banking and industrial conglom[eration] that monopolized large portions of the Japanese economy,"[25] which led to a paradigm that favored small and medium-sized companies and businesses. Yet even as small business responded to consumer demands and thrived in doing so, there lacked overarching guidelines to direct the economy as a whole.[26]

General MacArthur addressed this situation with the prime minister by stating the necessity to pursue "an integrated approach across the entire economic front," effectively stating "by SCAP that in the existing situation it was essential that 'free enterprise' should be replaced by a directed economy."[27] The result was a program termed "priority production," which allocated "labor and scare resources to key industrial sectors; direct[ed] government subsidies to those sectors; and [provided] policy-guided loans through a newly created Reconstruction Finance Bank."[28] While priority production developed a system that was rife with corruption, it managed to yield significant gains in targeted sectors and "focused attention on the critical heavy and chemical industrial sectors, instituted the postwar cult of top-level industrial policy making, bridged or fused a variety of economic ideologies, and brought the government and big business into an ever-closer embrace."[29]

---

[25] Rogers, "The Interagency Process in Reconstruction of Post-World War II Japan," 186.

[26] Dower, *Embracing Defeat: Japan in the Wake of World War II*, 533-4.

[27] W. Macmahon Ball, *Japan: Enemy or Ally?* (New York: John Day, 1949), 60-63, as quoted in Dower, 534.

[28] Dower, *Embracing Defeat: Japan in the Wake of World War II*, 534-5.

[29] Ibid., 536.

Although the seeds for success for a growing Japanese economy had been sown, the economy remained largely stagnant. An environmental change had to occur first before the potential of the newly demilitarized Japanese economic system could be realized.

The Korean War provided the necessary environmental change. The United States almost immediately depended on Japanese manufacturing to support the war effort on the Korean Peninsula and poured and estimated $2.3 billion into the Japanese economy from 1950 through 1953 – an amount that surpassed the total amount of aid received from the United States between 1945 and 1951.[30]

> Various indices convey a sense of this heady economic revival. A stagnant stock market rose 80 percent between the outbreak of war and December 1950. Steel production increased some 38 percent in the first eight months of the war, while steel exports tripled. The automobile industry was revived by large U.S. purchases of truck and other vehicles. This was the beginning of Japan's systematic acquisition of rights to American commercial licenses and patents – an immensely beneficial transaction that the U.S. government strongly supported as crucial for the economic well-being of still-fragile Cold War associate.[31]

The economic impact of the Korean War and its immediate aftermath was indeed "a gift of the Gods" to the Japanese economy.

Postwar Japan Stability Operations: Summary

This brief study of postwar Japan bears evidence to the complexity involved with stability operations in the wake of major combat operations. Even in a situation dominated by the efforts of American occupational activities, governance and development activities proved challenging at the very least. And even under the close and directive control of American and Japanese entities, the Japanese economy was

---

[30] Ibid., 542.

[31] Ibid.

31

unable to right itself until the regional economic system was radically altered by the onset of the Korean War.

Although current stability operations doctrine is not driven by American experiences of postwar Japan, one can see definite parallels between current doctrine and historical events. A brief cross-examination of the Potsdam Proclamation's objectives with the Stability Operations functions outlined in JP 3-07 show remarkable similarities:

- The military disarmament of Japan with the Security function
- The return of occupied territories with the Security function
- The bringing justice to war criminals with the Rule of Law function
- The strengthening democracy with the Governance and Participation function
- The economic demilitarization with the Economic Stabilization and Infrastructure function

It is also instructive to note that the U.S. whole-of-government approach was largely handled in Washington, giving General MacArthur supreme commander authorities in theater without a provision for transition to U.S. civil authorities. The postwar mission in Japan was a military mission from start to finish – which is counter to current doctrinal practices – but ensured both unity of command and unity of effort for the duration of the mission. Also of note is the length of time required to plan postwar stability operations, highlighting the complexity and effort required to comprehensively plan stability operations in the wake of major combat operations.

Counterinsurgency: Philippines

Few are likely to dispute the importance of stability operations in the aftermath of major combat. The direct destructive effects of combat are readily visible and demand a concerted effort. As they apply to a counterinsurgency (COIN) campaign, stability operations typically take a decidedly different approach as they are conducted simultaneously and in the same area of operations as offensive and defensive operations. "COIN requires joint forces to both fight and build sequentially or simultaneously, depending on the circumstances. Stability operations are fundamental to COIN – stability operations are the 'build' in the COIN process of 'clear, hold, build.'"[32] Where the conclusion to major combat operations marks the major shift in effort to stability and reconstruction efforts,[33] during a counterinsurgency campaign stability operations have an enduring characteristic, making them inextricably linked to the entire campaign plan. An instructive historical example of stability operations in a COIN environment is the United States' involvement in the Philippines from 1898 through 1902.

The context of the United States' involvement in the Philippines is dominated by the conduct of the Spanish-American War. Under the direction of then Assistant Secretary of the Navy Theodore Roosevelt, Commodore George Dewey attacked and decimated a portion of the Spanish fleet in Manila Bay.[34] As U.S. forces landed ashore to secure the surrender of Spanish forces, they found that the Spanish had been fighting a native uprising for the past two years. Led by Emilio Aguinaldo y Famy, Philippine rebel forces turned their attention toward the U.S. Army, perceiving that imperialism under the Americans was equally unacceptable as it was under the Spanish. The U.S. Navy's victory in Manila Bay was initially followed by similar successes on land as Aguinaldo's rebels attacked the U.S. forces conventionally, a tactic that won them bloody losses,

---

[32] JP 3-07, I-6.

[33] Ibid., I-5.

[34] Max Boot, *The Savage Wars of Peace: Small Wars and the Rise of American Power,* (New York: Basic Books, 2002), 103.

forced their retreat to the northern region of Luzon, and changed their strategy to that of a guerilla war.[35]

The Philippine War generally manifested itself in two phases of an insurgent-counterinsurgent conflict from 1900 through 1902. The first phase was in 1900 and was conducted under a policy thrust forth by President McKinley known as "benevolent assimilation." Benevolence – an early version of modern day "winning hearts and minds" – also became a guiding principle of how the U.S. Army conducted its operations.[36] McKinley's policy was of significance as it required the U.S. Army to conduct operations as a fighting force and establish and maintain a military government.

> In order to follow it, army officers would have to devote at least as much attention to civic projects, public works, government, and education as they would to military operations. In pursuit of the enemy, they must never lose sight of their responsibilities as representatives of American values or of their obligations to support and protect those who had submitted to the nation's authority.[37]

During this phase U.S. operations started with a concerted effort to improve the conditions in Manila by improving commerce, infrastructure, health and welfare, and education within the city.[38] These acts were complimented by offensive operations to isolate and destroy the insurgents. Major General Elwell Otis, the commanding officer of U.S. forces in the Philippines, established his counterinsurgency strategy under McKinley's policy of benevolence with a heavy focus on civic action. His strategy was

---

[35] Ibid.

[36] Brian McAllister Linn, *The Philippine War, 1899-1902,* (Lawrence, Kansas: University Press of Kansas, 2000), 30.

[37] Ibid., 31.

[38] These actions fit neatly into today's stability functions of Economic Stabilization and Infrastructure and Humanitarian Assistance.

simple: once the Filipinos experience the benefits brought about by American rule, they would shift their support from the rebels to the Americans.[39]

As Otis handed command of the war effort to General Arthur MacArthur in the summer of 1900, MacArthur continued Otis' strategy, focusing on the establishment and administration of civic-centered projects. U.S. civil-military efforts were also in place early in the war as General MacArthur was teamed with William Howard Taft, who was appointed "as chairman of a commission to supervise the transition from military to civilian rule in pacified areas."[40] Under this system Taft also focused on a policy of benevolence, further emphasizing construction efforts to "win over" the support of the Philippine population, an approach that met with mixed results.

A key turning point in the war was the United States' election of 1900. Aguinaldo had escalated attacks on American forces to increase negative press with the American population with hopes that anti-imperialist William Jennings Bryan would be elected President.[41] Aguinaldo's efforts failed and McKinley was reelected President, enabling MacArthur and his 69,000 veteran troops to change their strategy to one of a "Policy of Chastisement."[42]

U.S. forces shifted to a policy of chastisement for several reasons, primarily spurred by the realization that the policy of benevolence alone was insufficient to win the war. A pertinent factor was certainly that tensions rose between American soldiers and Filipino civilians because of racial issues and soldier misconduct. Added to this, U.S.

---

[39] Ibid., 200.

[40] Boot, *The Savage Wars of Peace: Small Wars and the Rise of American Power,* 114.

[41] Andrew J. Birtle, *U.S. Army Counterinsurgency and Contingency Operations Doctrine 1860-1941,* (Washington DC: U.S. Government Printing Office, 1997), 112.

[42] Ibid., 126.

leadership had underestimated the strength and will of the insurgency; this was not a superficial uprising that could be rapidly quelled.[43] Lastly, the U.S. policy of benevolence largely failed because of the brutality that the insurgents imposed on the population. "Until the American could convince the people that they were strong enough to protect their friends and punish their enemies, the Filipinos saw little reason to risk their lives for 'Uncle Sam.'"[44]

Chastisement brought harsher wartime practices for Aguinaldo, his rebel forces, and the Philippine population. Reminiscent of Sherman's march across Georgia, MacArthur's new strategy proved very compelling.

> Indeed, devastation, not just selective retaliatory burnings but the complete destruction of sections of countryside, soon became a hallmark of the counterinsurgency campaign. The scope and intensity of Army incendiary operations varied throughout the archipelago depending on the degree of resistance and the inclinations of local commanders. In their most extreme form they entailed the obliteration for entire areas deemed to be under guerrilla control or strongly sympathetic to the resistance. In such sectors the Army put to the torch homes, villages, storehouses, orchards, crops, livestock, boats, and even fishing nets. By destroying entire areas, field commanders hoped to give the surrounding regions an object lesson in American power that would encourage insurgency collaborators to reconsider their position. More important, devastation was part of the wider military strategy to beat the guerrillas into submission by eliminating all food and shelter in their base areas.[45]

Brutal as it may seem by today's standards, the policy of chastisement ended up playing a winning hand in the war. Not only did it prove to directly apply pressure the rebel forces, it also directly addressed the problem of tacit support by the Philippine population. In the end, it was the combination of chastisement with benevolence that ended up delivering the American victory to the war.

---

[43] Ibid., 125.

[44] Ibid., 126.

[45] Ibid., 129.

It was only when they [the rebels] had been pushed to the brink that the policy of [benevolence] had played a significant role in bringing about the end of the insurrection, for at this point benevolence helped to reconcile the remaining insurgents to defeat. This was especially so because, by accident rather than by design, America's program of moderate political reforms, economic growth, and education, appealed to the conservative leaders of the Filipino insurrection.[46]

This example presents the importance of both combat and stability forces in a counterinsurgency campaign. Neither in and of itself is sufficient to bring about a successful end to the conflict. Without combat forces the enemy remains unconfronted and enjoys freedom of movement and action in the battle space, necessitating adequate security measures in the OE. Without stability forces there is little to attract the support of the population, which is the main objective in a counterinsurgency fight. It is the proper balance of stability and combat forces in a COIN fight that is of ultimate importance.

Counterinsurgency Stability Operations in the Philippines: Summary

Similar to the previous case study of postwar Japan, the operational environment faced by U.S. forces in the Philippines was very complex. Yet differing significantly from General Douglas MacArthur's situation in dealing with an enemy that had accepted an unconditional surrender, both General Otis and General Arthur MacArthur had to balance combat and stability operations in order to eventually bring about a successful end to the war.

When comparing the U.S. experiences in the Philippine war with current stability operations doctrine, linkages to the stability functions are not as clear as those identified in postwar Japan. However, under the policy of benevolence U.S. forces concentrated on Economic Stabilization and Infrastructure and Governance and Participation functions.

---

[46] Ibid., 135.

As the policy shifted to one of chastisement, the Security function initially dominated the American approach to the war with subsequent increases in the other four functions as the insurgent forces were isolated and defeated.

Historical Examples Analysis

This chapter briefly outlined two historical stability operations campaigns in an attempt to build the reader's understanding of the complexity and importance of stability operations. Additionally, it underscores the importance of stability operations in the context of both major combat and counterinsurgency operations. But what is one to glean from these two examples that may be applicable today?

First, it is important to understand that stability operations are equally important to both major combat and counterinsurgency operations. In either situation, the imperative "to maintain or reestablish a safe and secure environment, provide essential government services, emergency infrastructure reconstruction, and humanitarian relief" falls to the DOD.[47] Indeed, it is difficult for one to imagine any conflict where the United States is or has been involved and where U.S. forces were to return home and leave behind the war-torn remnants of a state; the world's outcry at such an act would certainly be deafening.[48]

Second, although they have the same fundamental functions, stability operations in a COIN environment are employed in a very different manner than their corresponding efforts in major combat operations. In the context of a counterinsurgency, stability operations take shape immediately and enhance, reinforce, and exploit the successes that

---

[47] U.S. Department of Defense, *DoD Instruction 3000.05*, 1.

[48] Since their establishment during WWII, Civil Affairs units have traditionally been employed to conduct stability operations. For in-depth information on the composition and employment of Civil Affairs forces, see Joint Publication 3-57, *Civil-Military Operations*, dated 08 July 2008.

combat forces provide. The parallel efforts of combat and stability forces enable a synergistic effect by simultaneously engaging and influencing the population and the enemy, but the presence of ongoing combat operations makes stability operations in a COIN environment particularly challenging. One is at risk of mismatching combat and stability efforts if proper coordination is not accomplished.

By contrast, when stability operations are conducted as part of a major combat operations type of conflict, they typically are planned during the course of the conflict and are undertaken at the conclusion of major combat. Thus when stability forces are employed in the aftermath of major combat operations, the weight of effort is stability operations focused.

Third, whether stability operations are performed in the context of a counterinsurgency or major combat campaign, they require a massive coordination effort in order to ensure that they are properly nested with other coalition efforts, international organizations, and host nation forces and organizations. It is important to remain focused on the end state of stability operations: the transition of control to host nation entities and the subsequent withdrawal of U.S. forces, highlighting that stability operations forces build the host nation capacity and capability, which in turn enable U.S. forces' withdrawal.

CHAPTER 3: AFGHANISTAN PROVINCIAL RECONSTRUCTION TEAMS

PRTs build on capabilities previously established, but represent a new step in the evolution of interagency coordination. In a way not seen since Vietnam, military and civilian government officials are working side-by-side in the field to ensure unity of effort in meeting our national objectives.[1]

In the context of the war in Afghanistan, one tool that the United States and several coalition nations have implemented in order to enable troop withdrawal is the Provincial Reconstruction Team (PRT). PRTs are civil-military (CIV-MIL) organizations assembled to operate in semi-permissive operating environments in order to help the host nation build its capacity and effectiveness.[2] PRTs employ an approach that includes diplomatic, military, and development components to enable stabilization and reconstruction efforts.[3] Envisioned as a hub of U.S. government (USG) and international assistance efforts in Afghanistan, PRTs focus on local government improvements, improving security and rule of law, and reconstruction efforts.[4]

The United States' ongoing efforts in Afghanistan are marked by significant PRT contributions in conducting stability operations. US PRTs were first introduced into Afghanistan in 2002 in the city of Gardez, Paktia Province in order to centralize the execution of security, governance, and development initiatives at the provincial level.[5] Since then the US PRT footprint has grown to include 13 PRTs in the provinces of

---

[1] Major General Jason K. Kamiya, Preface to *Provincial Reconstruction Teams*, Pre-doctrinal Research White Paper No. 07-01, (U.S. Joint Forces Command, November 21, 2007), 3.

[2] Center for Army Lessons Learned, *Afghanistan Provincial Reconstruction Team,* 1.

[3] Ibid., 2.

[4] Ibid., 5.

[5] J. Edward Fox, "Preparing Civilians for Deployment to Civilian-Military Platforms in Combat Environments: The Evolution of Staffing and Training for the Civilian Mission in Afghanistan," in *Towards a Comprehensive Approach: Strategic and Operational Challenges*, ed. Christopher M. Schnaubelt, (Rome: NATO Defense College, May 2011), 43.

Panjshir, Nuristan, Kunar, Laghman, Nangarhar, Paktiya, Khost, Paktika, Ghazni, Zabul, Kandahar, Farah, and Uruzgan. Coalition partner nations operate an additional 14 PRTs from 13 different partner nations.[6] The coalition PRTs operate in Kunduz & Badakhshan (Germany), Balkh (Sweden), Baghlan (Hungary), Faryab (Norway), Jawzjan (Turkey), Herat (Italy), Badghis (Spain), Ghor (Lithuania), Helmand (United Kingdom), Bamyan (Australia), Wardak (Turkey), Parwan (South Korea), and Logar (Czech Republic) provinces.[7]

Concept of Operations

As described in JP 3-07, in the continuum of offensive, defensive, and stability operations, host-nation capability deficits can prevent a steady transition from primarily offensive and defensive operations to primarily stability operations. As this evolution progresses, effort is required to enhance the government's ability to provide for the population, yet the lack of security necessitates a component to enable a level of security that facilitates governance and development advances.[8] This effort is usually filled by a military force during the initial stages but may also be filled by a police or paramilitary force. PRTs were specifically designed and fielded to operate in these pockets of instability to establish sustainable host-nation capabilities and facilitate the withdrawal of military forces in lieu of more traditional diplomatic and development approaches.[9]

A PRT's mission is initially focused on assessing the operational environment (OE), gaining access to key host-nation security and governance institutions, performing

---

[6] International Security Assistance Force website, http://www.nato.int/isaf/docu/epub/pdf/placemat.pdf (accessed March 14, 2012).

[7] Ibid.

[8] Center for Army Lessons Learned, *Afghanistan Provincial Reconstruction Team*, 6.

[9] Ibid.

integrated campaign planning, and implementing the integrated campaign plan.[10] During

execution of the campaign plan and with the occurrence of force rotations into and out of

theater, the PRT's initial approach changes to include active review and adjustments of

the campaign plan. This creates a continuum of tension that must balance efforts marked

by continuity with flexibility that can alter operations as aspects of the OE change over

time.[11] To achieve this balance, the teams establish and strive toward objectives to

"improve stability, increase local institutional capacity, facilitate reconstruction activities,

and execute a strong strategic communications program."[12]

PRTs set their objectives based upon guidance that they receive from multiple

agencies at multiple levels. Although Afghanistan PRTs primary guidance comes from

the International Security Assistance Force (ISAF), PRT's CIV-MIL structure combined

with necessary coordination with host-nation and other national, international, and non-

governmental agencies/organizations results in disparate, often conflicting, sets of

implementation guidance and objectives that all converge at the PRT.[13]

This defines the nexus of operations for the PRT, and to achieve success in the

OE, PRTs must build a plan that accurately addresses the causes of instability,

accommodates disparate guidance from multiple agencies, implements a multi-year

approach that provides continuity of effort across multiple combat rotations, and

maximizes the synergistic effects available with an interagency team.[14] In both planning

and execution, teams must ensure accurate measures of performance and effectiveness

---

[10] Ibid., 8.

[11] Ibid., 11.

[12] Ibid., 12.

[13] Ibid., 19.

[14] Ibid., 22-23.

that are linked to the team's operations. Because much of the PRT's efforts are focused on medium and long-term improvements, measuring effectiveness is often very difficult and prompts a tendency to measure performance rather than effectiveness.[15] Again, this underscores the necessity for a long-term campaign plan and an approach of continuity that spans multiple combat rotations. "Without a long-term plan, new arrivals are left to improvise their own programs, drawing on their own expertise, which results in choppy and ineffective PRT programming and wastes time and resources."[16]

PRT Laghman

Provincial Reconstruction Team Laghman is in the Regional Command East (RC(E)) area of operations and is located in eastern Afghanistan, between Kabul and the Pakistan border. Laghman's topography is a mix of mountainous and flat terrain that is dominated by the confluence of the Alishing, Alingar, and Kabul rivers, providing Laghman with greater than average water resources.[17] Pashtuns constitute the largest portion of Laghman's population of just under 400,000, and agriculture, day labor, and government employment dominate the province's job market.[18] Because of Laghman's location on Highway 7, the main thoroughfare between Kabul and Pakistan, Laghman is subject to significant levels of violence, primarily as a result of the activities of the

---

[15] Ibid., 27.

[16] Ibid., 28.

[17] Program of Culture & Conflict Studies, "Laghman Province," http://www.nps.edu/programs/ccs/Docs/Executive%20Summaries/Laghman_Provincial_Overview_CCS.pdf, (accessed February 25, 2012).

[18] Ibid.

Taliban and HIG[19] (Hezb-e Islami Gulbuddin), who use Laghman as a transit ground to and from other provinces.

The city of Mehtar Lam is Laghman's provincial capital, and is also home to U.S. forces at Forward Operating Base (FOB) Mehtar Lam. U.S. forces based at FOB Mehtar Lam include an infantry battalion (FOB and battle space owner), the Kansas Agri-business Development Team (ADT), and PRT Laghman. All of these units are aligned under ISAF's RC(E) chain of command and share the same battle space.[20]

The remainder of this chapter analyzes PRT Laghman's mission statement and commander's intent statement. It continues by studying aspects of the PRT Laghman's organization and personnel structure and the nuances associated with the PRT's command and control, both internal and external to the unit. The chapter's analysis concludes with studying the financial tools available to the unit in its conduct of stability operations.

Mission and Intent

As described in JP 5-0, as an organization conducts mission analysis as part of the Joint Operation Planning Process (JOPP), the planning team establishes the units' proposed mission statement and commander's intent statement.[21] These documents

---

[19] The HIG is a Mujahideen party that has been active since the Soviet invasion. It is led by Gulbuddin Hekmatyar, and is actively opposed to US-led and Afghan national forces. http://www.nps.edu/programs/ccs/Laghman.html (accessed February 25, 2012).

[20] RC-East website, http://www.isaf.nato.int/subordinate-commands/rc-east/index.php, (accessed February 25, 2012). Per the website, "RC-East includes the provinces of: Bamyan, Ghazni, Kapisa, Khost, Kunar, Laghman, Logar, Nangarhar, Nuristan, Paktika Paktiya, Panjshayr, Parwan and Wardak provinces. Regional Command-East is made up of 14 provinces covering 43,000 square miles, approximately the size of Ohio and sharing 450 miles of border with Pakistan. Currently, more than 30,150 Coalition forces from 13 nations and 850 civilians are deployed in RC-E."

[21] U.S. Joint Chiefs of Staff, *Joint Operation Planning*, IV-5.

provide an instructive tool to help understand what PRTs accomplish in the battle space and why they do it. In this endeavor this paper analyzes PRT Laghman's mission and intent from the 2010-2011 combat rotation. In order to better understand the context of PRT Laghman's mission and intent, it is worthwhile to briefly examine and analyze the mission statement and commander's intent from higher echelons. At the beginning of the Operation Enduring Freedom (OEF) XI-XII combat rotation, Regional Command-East (RC(E)) was led by the 101st Airborne Division which comprised Combined Joint Task Force 101 (CJTF-101). The CJTF-101 mission statement is outlined in Figure 3:[22]

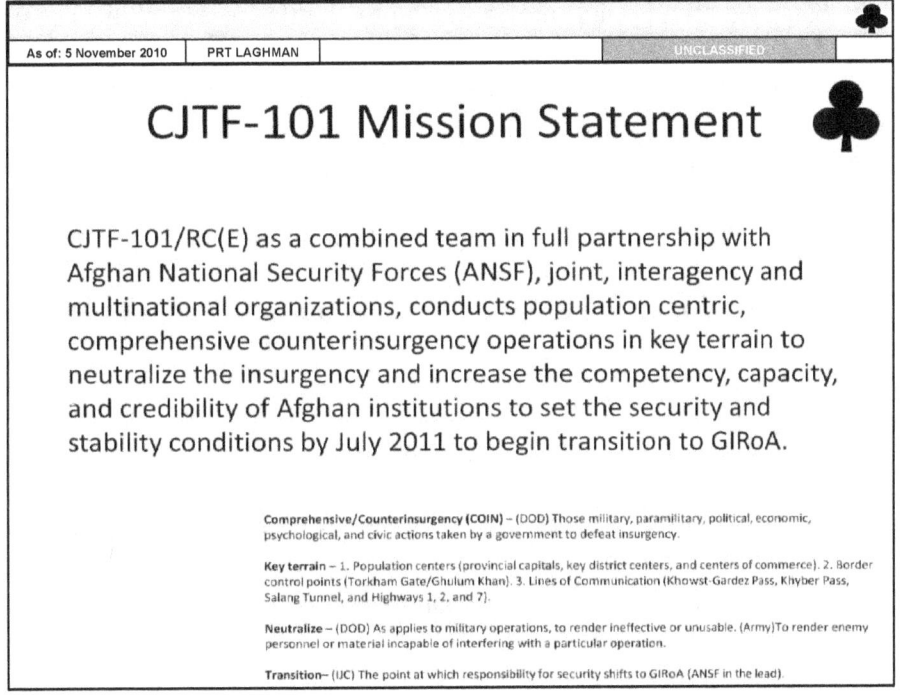

Figure 3: CJTF-101/RC(E) Mission Statement.[23]

The RC(E) mission statement is instructive in several ways. First, it provides a recent example of the stated focus of a division-level headquarters in a COIN

---

[22] CJTF-101, RC(E) Mission Briefing, (5 November 2010), 8. Acronyms used: CJTF – Combined Joint Task Force; GIRoA – Government of the Islamic Republic of Afghanistan.

[23] Ibid.

environment. The conduct of "comprehensive counterinsurgency operations" implies that the force will determine and maintain the delicate balance of offensive, defensive, and stability operations. When viewed through the lens of JP 3-07's stability functions, "neutralize the insurgency" is clearly a security function, while "increase the competency, capacity, and credibility of Afghan institutions" applies to Humanitarian Assistance, Economic Stabilization and Infrastructure, Rule of Law, and Governance and Participation functions. The explicit inclusion of Afghan National Security Forces (ANSF) and joint, interagency and multinational organizations makes clear that the unit's focus is to be balanced among multiple entities in the battle space and implies that a significant effort will be made to integrate operations with these entities. It also states that the focus of operations is in key terrain, which plays hand-in-hand with the population-centric counterinsurgency strategy. Within this strategy, key terrain is codified by a system of Key Terrain Districts, and lasting results and ultimate mission success emerges from increasing "the competency, capacity, and credibility of Afghan institutions." This leads to a second instructive point in that the importance of stability operations in the context of a larger COIN effort, or perhaps the inextricable linkages between stability operations and COIN combat operations (as was noted in the Philippines), is clearly stated.

This mission statement is further refined by the CJTF-101 Commander's Intent, as outlined in Figure 4:

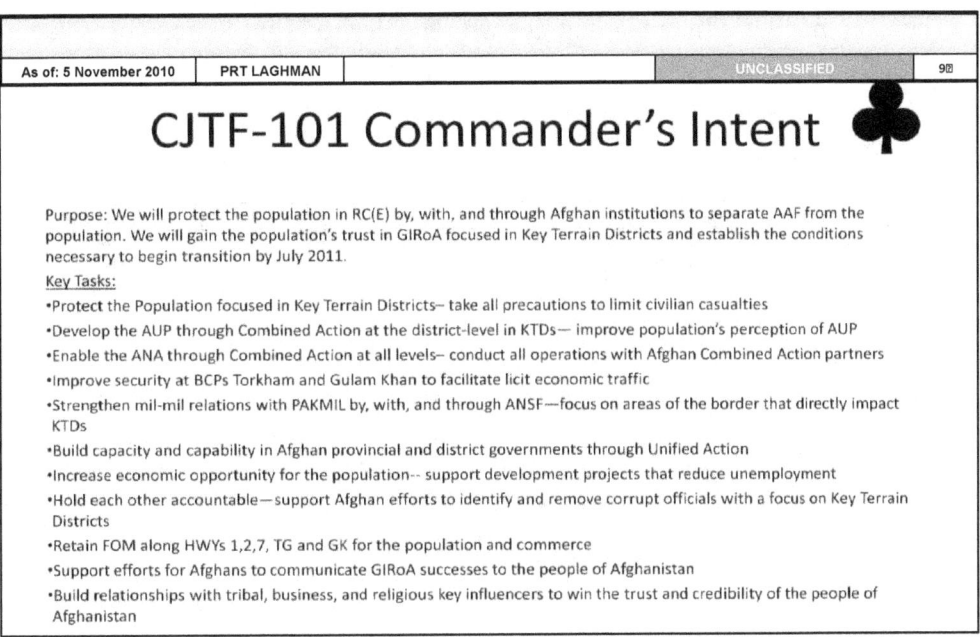

CJTF-101 Commander's Intent ♣

Purpose: We will protect the population in RC(E) by, with, and through Afghan institutions to separate AAF from the population. We will gain the population's trust in GIRoA focused in Key Terrain Districts and establish the conditions necessary to begin transition by July 2011.

Key Tasks:

• Protect the Population focused in Key Terrain Districts– take all precautions to limit civilian casualties
• Develop the AUP through Combined Action at the district-level in KTDs– improve population's perception of AUP
• Enable the ANA through Combined Action at all levels– conduct all operations with Afghan Combined Action partners
• Improve security at BCPs Torkham and Gulam Khan to facilitate licit economic traffic
• Strengthen mil-mil relations with PAKMIL by, with, and through ANSF—focus on areas of the border that directly impact KTDs
• Build capacity and capability in Afghan provincial and district governments through Unified Action
• Increase economic opportunity for the population-- support development projects that reduce unemployment
• Hold each other accountable—support Afghan efforts to identify and remove corrupt officials with a focus on Key Terrain Districts
• Retain FOM along HWYs 1,2,7, TG and GK for the population and commerce
• Support efforts for Afghans to communicate GIRoA successes to the people of Afghanistan
• Build relationships with tribal, business, and religious key influencers to win the trust and credibility of the people of Afghanistan

Figure 4: CJTF-101/RC(E) Commander's Intent.[24]

"A concise expression of the purpose of the operation and the desired end state,"[25] the Commander's Intent adds another level of fidelity to the planning and conduct of operations in the OE. Similar to the mission statement, the RC(E) Commander's Intent is instructive when viewed through the lens of JP 3-07's security functions. The Commander's stated purpose explicitly balances security and governance efforts in preparation for transition [to civil authorities] activities in 2011. The first five key tasks are exclusively Security focused, while the remaining tasks balance Governance and Participation, Rule of law, and Economic Stabilization and Infrastructure.

---

[24] Ibid., 9. Acronyms used: AAF – Anti-Afghan Forces; AUP – Afghan Uniformed Police; KTD – Key Terrain District; ANA – Afghan National Army; BCP – Border Control Point; PAKMIL – Pakistani Military; FOM – Freedom of Movement; TG – Torkham Gate; GK – Gulam Khan.

[25] U.S. Joint Chiefs of Staff, *Department of Defense Dictionary of Military and Associated Terms*, Joint Publication 1-02, (Washington DC: Joint Chiefs of Staff, May 15, 2011), 67.

The Commander's Intent concludes with the desired End State, which is outlined

in Figure 5:

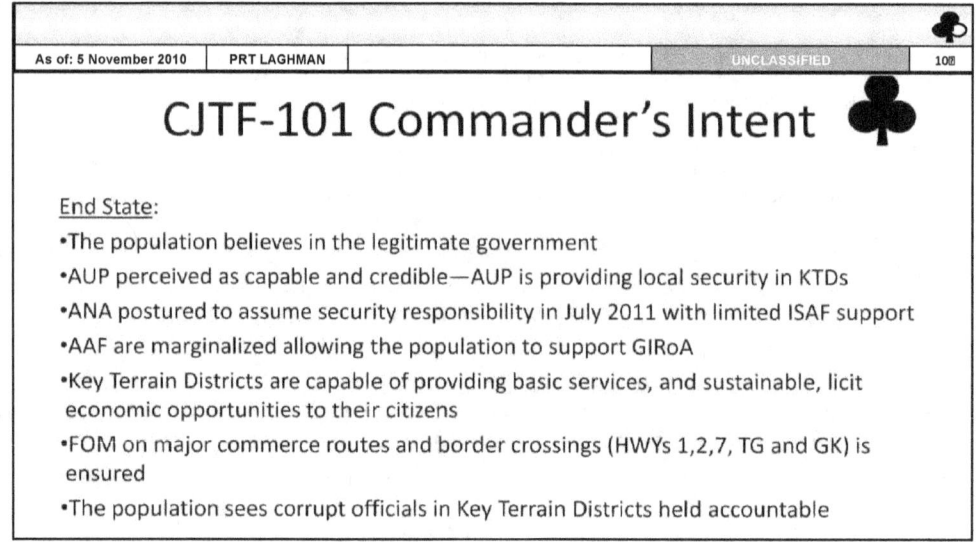

Figure 5: CJTF-101/RC(E) Commander's Intent.[26]

"The set of required conditions that defines achievement of the commander's

objectives," the Commander's desired end state conditions are also easily categorized by

JP 3-07's stability functions as shown below:

- Population believes in the government (Governance and Participation)
- AUP perceived as capable and credible (Security)
- ANA postured for responsibility (Security)
- AAF are marginalized (Security)
- Key Terrain Districts provide for the population (Economic Stabilization and Infrastructure, Governance and Participation, and Rule of Law)
- FOM on major commerce routes (Security)
- Corrupt officials held accountable (Rule of Law)

Derived from and nesting with the RC(E) mission statement and commander's

intent, PRT Laghman's mission statement and commander's intent are illustrated in

Figure 6 and are discussed below.[27]

---

[26] Ibid., 10.

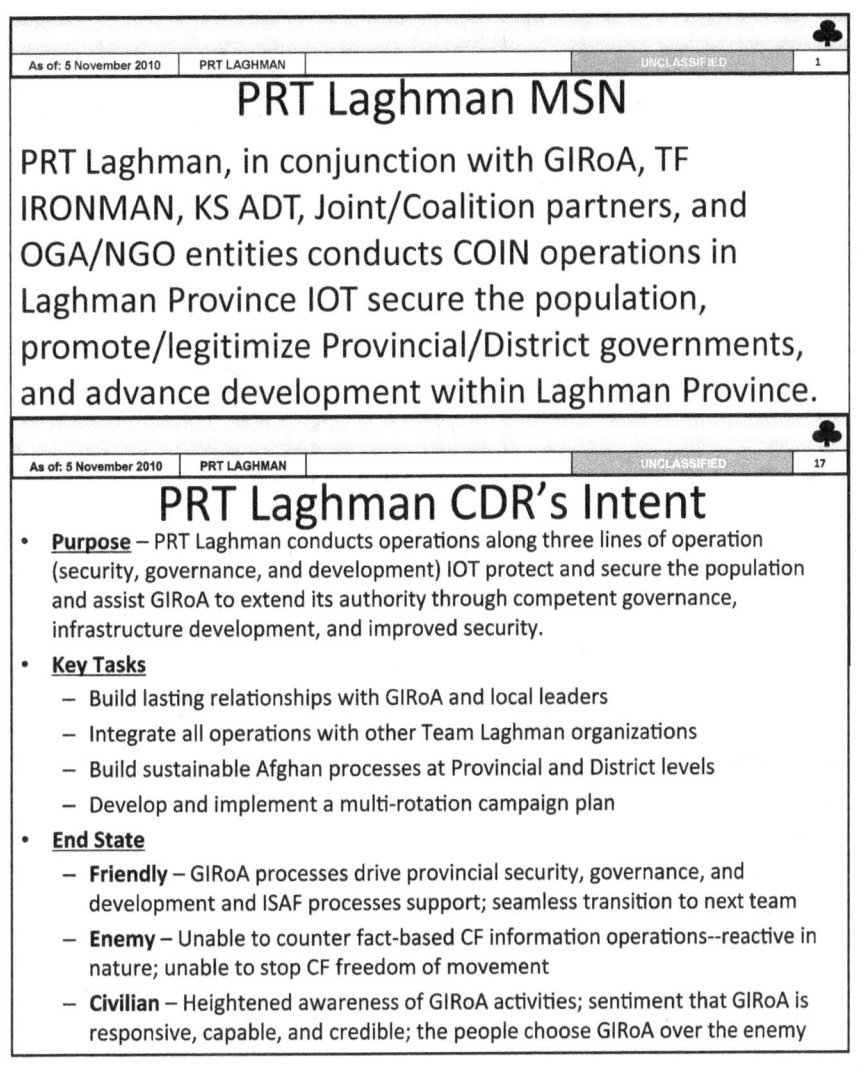

As of: 5 November 2010   PRT LAGHMAN   UNCLASSIFIED   1

PRT Laghman MSN

PRT Laghman, in conjunction with GIRoA, TF IRONMAN, KS ADT, Joint/Coalition partners, and OGA/NGO entities conducts COIN operations in Laghman Province IOT secure the population, promote/legitimize Provincial/District governments, and advance development within Laghman Province.

As of: 5 November 2010   PRT LAGHMAN   UNCLASSIFIED   17

PRT Laghman CDR's Intent

- **Purpose** – PRT Laghman conducts operations along three lines of operation (security, governance, and development) IOT protect and secure the population and assist GIRoA to extend its authority through competent governance, infrastructure development, and improved security.
- **Key Tasks**
  - Build lasting relationships with GIRoA and local leaders
  - Integrate all operations with other Team Laghman organizations
  - Build sustainable Afghan processes at Provincial and District levels
  - Develop and implement a multi-rotation campaign plan
- **End State**
  - **Friendly** – GIRoA processes drive provincial security, governance, and development and ISAF processes support; seamless transition to next team
  - **Enemy** – Unable to counter fact-based CF information operations--reactive in nature; unable to stop CF freedom of movement
  - **Civilian** – Heightened awareness of GIRoA activities; sentiment that GIRoA is responsive, capable, and credible; the people choose GIRoA over the enemy

Figure 6: PRT Laghman Mission Statement and Commander's Intent.[28]

As one would expect, there are clear similarities between the RC(E) and PRT Laghman

mission statements and commander's intent statements. As seen in Figure 6, PRT

Laghman's efforts focused on the Governance and Participation, Rule of Law, and

Economic Stabilization and Infrastructure stability functions. Also of note is that the

---

[27] 1st Brigade Combat Team (BCT), 101st Airborne Division (AASLT) was PRT Laghman's operational control (OPCON) brigade at the beginning of PRT Laghman's OEF XI-XII combat rotation.

[28] Ibid. Acronyms used: TF – Task Force; KS ADT – Kansas Agribusiness Development Team; OGA – Other Government Agency; NGO – Non-Government Agency; COIN – Counterinsurgency; IOT – In Order To; ISAF – International Security Assistance Force; CF – Coalition Force.

Commander's Intent references three lines of operation, which were set forth in the International Security Assistance Force (ISAF) counterinsurgency campaign plan.[29] ISAF's three lines of operation – security, governance, and reconstruction[30] neatly correspond to the Security, Governance and Participation, and Economic Stabilization and Infrastructure stability functions, respectively.

It becomes clear after analyzing PRT Laghman's mission and commander's intent statements that the PRT's aim is to conduct stability operations. The following pages analyze how the PRT is organized and manned to conduct this mission.

Organization and Personnel

Finding qualified individuals with applicable skills and experience poses a significant challenge to staffing PRTs. Civilian agencies have not had capacity to surge to fill the increased number of PRTs in Iraq or the few civilian PRT positions in Afghanistan, and they may not have the rotational base to continue staffing these teams into the future. The Department of Defense has provided the vast majority of PRT personnel, including both civilian and military members, but it has had challenges providing personnel with appropriate skills.[31]

PRTs are unique in that their CIV-MIL personnel structure combined with unique military skill sets enables them to focus on stability operations functions. The vast majority of PRT personnel are military, most of which provide movement and security functions to enable operations in semi-permissive environments. PRT's also have key military and civilian personnel that equip the unit well in its conduct of stability operations. As displayed in Figure 7, PRT Laghman is organized with a traditional staff structure whereby staff sections are individually aligned under the command element. Depicted in the figure are the staff sections with individual positions identified with rank

---

[29] Major General Kasdorf, 1.

[30] Ibid.

[31] U.S. House of Representatives, *Agency Stovepipes vs Strategic Agility*, 25.

and service/department. Figure 7 also annotates the command relationships within the

unit by either a solid line (operational control) or dashed line (tactical control).[32]

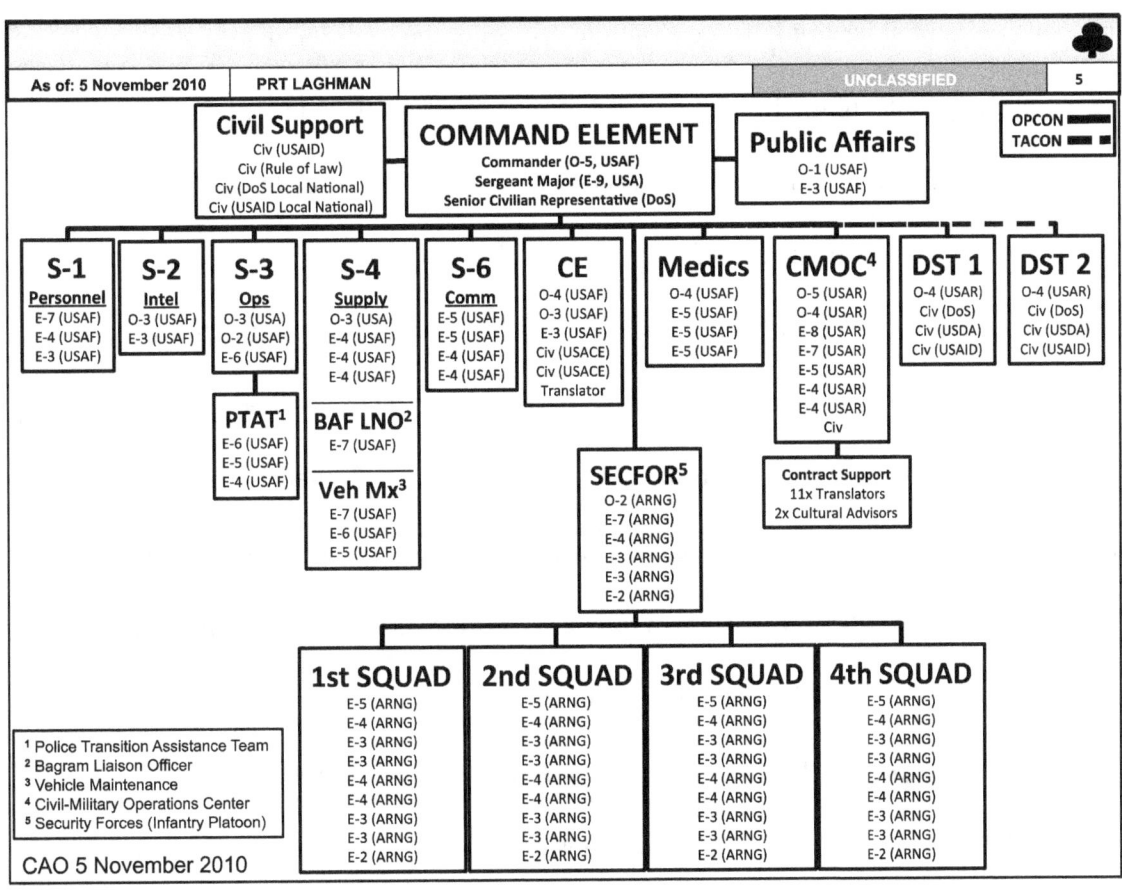

Figure 7: PRT Laghman Organization Chart[33]

Figure 7 highlights several points. First is the integrated civil-military nature of

the PRT. The inclusion of Department of State (DOS), United States Aid and

International Development (USAID), and United States Department of Agriculture

(USDA) personnel adds significant capability and credibility to the PRT in its conduct of

---

[32] As defined by JP 1-02, "Operational Control is the authority to perform those functions of command over subordinate forces involving organizing and employing commands and forces, assigning tasks, designating objectives, and giving authoritative direction necessary to accomplish the mission." Also as defined by JP 1-02, Tactical control is the "Command authority over assigned or attached forces or commands, or military capability or forces made available for tasking, that is limited to the detailed direction and control of movements or maneuvers within the operational area necessary to accomplish missions or tasks assigned." U.S. Joint Chiefs of Staff, *Departement of Defense Dictionary of Military and Associated Terms*, 270, 359.

[33] PRT Laghman, PRT Laghman Command Briefing, (5 November 2010), 5.

stability operations. The inclusion of United States Government civilians in the PRT

provides the unit with expertise, funding, and reach-back capabilities that would not be

possible with a military-only force structure. Second, the traditional staff structure

requires many conventionally trained military personnel to provide basic unit support

functions to enable specialized PRT mission execution. Examples of this are the S-1

(personnel), S-2 (intelligence), S-3 (operations), S-4 (logistics), and S-6

(communications). Third, a large portion of the PRT consists of an infantry platoon

security force (SECFOR) unit that conducts movement, protection, and security

operations for PRT missions. Fourth, and most importantly, is that the PRT has

specialized staff sections that conduct specific stability operations functions that make the

PRT unique in the battle space; these include the police transition assistance team

(PTAT), medical staff, civil engineers, civil-military operations center, and District

Support Teams (DSTs). Each of these is discussed in detail below.

Working closely with the battalion task forces' Security Force Assistance (SFA)

team, the PTAT performs train-the-trainer missions with Afghan National Police (ANP)

forces at the provincial and district levels.[34] In this role the PTAT conducts patrols with

the ANP, helps establish and implement ANP training plans, and conducts ANP training

courses for mid-level ANP personnel.[35] Working within the Security stability function

and linking to operations in the Governance and Participation and Rule of Law stability

---

[34] Captain Tony Vincelli, "Provincial Reconstruction Team Uses Infantry Soldiers to Bolster Joint Patrols," (1 September 2011), http://www.centcom.mil/news/provincial-reconstruction-team-uses-infantry-soldiers-to-bolster-joint-patrols (accessed February 25, 2012).

[35] Staff Sergeant Julie Weckerlein, "Afghans Train Afghans with American Mentorship," (11 September 2007), http://www.af.mil/news/story.asp?id=123067439 (accessed February 25, 2012).

functions, PTAT efforts directly work toward building lasting, competent indigenous Afghan police forces.[36]

The PRT medical staff personnel are primarily used for troop medical clinic duty and combat medic duty for mounted and dismounted combat patrols. Above and beyond their basic tasks, medical engagement with Afghan medical providers is a mission essential task for PRT medical personnel in the conduct of the Economic Stabilization and Infrastructure stability operations function. With the PRT lead medical officer as the primary contact with the provincial Ministry of Health line director, the PRT's medical personnel conduct health clinic assessments and coordinate for development and construction of medical clinics and hospitals.[37] PRT medical personnel also "facilitate medical training and mentorship for health care providers" and link with the PRT's civil engineer staff section to "refurbish medical care facilities."[38]

The PRT's civil engineering (CE) staff section constitutes a critical PRT capability by conducting the Economic Stabilization and Infrastructure stability operations function. Leveraging career education and training on structural, electrical, and construction engineering skill sets, the CE section works closely with the Ministry of Rural Rehabilitation and Development line director to "ensure the social, economic and political well-being of rural society."[39] In this role the PRT CE section works as a contracting agent representative for US-funded reconstruction projects, provides project

[36] Center for Army Lessons Learned, *Afghanistan Provincial Reconstruction Team,* 47.

[37] Staff Sergeant Ryan Crane, "PRT Laghman Visits Local Hospital," (24 August 2011), http://www.dvidshub.net/image/447204/prt-laghman-visits-local-hospital#.T0k6sJjPVUQ (accessed February 25, 2012).

[38] Center for Army Lessons Learned, *Afghanistan Provincial Reconstruction Team,* 47.

[39] Islamic Republic of Afghanistan, Ministry of Rural Rehabilitation & Development, http://mrrd.gov.af/en/page/67 (accessed September 29, 2011).

oversight through routine quality assurance/quality control (QA/QC) inspections, and closely coordinates with GIRoA officials to build GIRoA's capability and capacity to conduct reconstruction projects autonomously or with NGO support.[40] In a vein similar to that of the PTAT, the PRT CE section provides a critical long-term function by bridging the gap between current levels of indigenous government capability with an increased future capability that will allow US force withdrawal from the area of operations.

The PRT Civil-Military Operations Center (CMOC) consists of an Army Civil Affairs (CA) team augmented by civilian and local national contractor personnel. The CMOC provides several critical mission functions for the PRT. First, they conduct tactical CA functions on PRT missions. In this capacity a minimum of one CA Soldier is on every patrol to conduct consequence management operations in the event of an incident and to collect information from the local population. The CMOC also serves as the PRT Commander's Emergency Response Program (CERP) bulk funds management agent. In this capacity CMOC personnel coordinate with GIRoA officials to identify, coordinate, and fund small-scale, quick-impact stability operation projects in the area. The CMOC also serves as the PRT's counterinsurgency-centric planning and execution cell. By virtue of the career training and experiences of the CMOC's CA Soldiers, they provide invaluable insight on interfacing with the local population and local government agencies, the implementation of stability operations programs in the battle space, and

---

[40] U.S. Forces Afghanistan, *Money As A Weapon System (MAAWS-A)*, USFOR-A Pub 1-06, Commander's Emergency Respons Program (CERP) SOP, (February 2011), http://www.michaelyon-online.com/images/pdf/maaws-feb-2011-1.pdf (accessed February 25, 2012).

integrating PRT operations with other battle space users (e.g., adjacent units, NGOs, and OGAs).

As Civil Affairs personnel and the CMOC are central to PRT operations, it is fitting to highlight the value that the CA community brings to the execution of stability operations. While an in-depth discussion of CA is beyond the scope of this paper, CA personnel have the most relevant training and skill sets in the conduct of stability operations as associated with PRTs.[41]

Although they are not organic to the PRT, PRTs have tactical control over District Support Teams (DSTs). DSTs were formed to extend the reach of the PRT into previously unreachable areas at the district levels of Afghan government.[42] Typically operating with company-sized maneuver elements in the battle space, DSTs include civilian and military personnel that are assigned for a year or longer in order to build lasting relationships with district government officials. "DSTs seek to strengthen the district government's links with provincial authorities ensuring the needs of the district are conveyed and that appropriate ministries in Kabul address their needs."[43] DSTs are key to the evolving COIN strategy in Afghanistan and have been one target of President Obama's civilian "uplift" that increased the number of civilians in theater and dispersed many of them into the field, rather than retaining them on main operating bases and in large units.[44]

---

[41] U.S. House of Representatives, *Agency Stovepipes vs Strategic Agility,* 25.

[42] Center for Army Lessons Learned, *Afghanistan Provincial Reconstruction Team,* 47.

[43] Ibid.

[44] James Traub, "Afghanistan's Civic War," *The New York Times,* June 15, 2010.

The PRTs' disparate composition makes for a challenging situation for both military commanders and civilian leaders alike in that unity of command is rarely achieved and unity of effort is challenging, at best. Unfortunately, the command and control structures that link to PRTs tend to hamper rather than bolster PRT operations. The nuances of PRT command and control structures are discussed in the following pages.

Command and Control

Command and control varies with leadership of the teams and their related military command and civilian supervisors. Essentially, there are multiple chains of command: through the military, the Office of Provincial Affairs, the embassies, and Washington-based country representative of the departments and agencies. The PRTs thus lack clean lines of authority, and the coordination procedures between civilian and military personnel are disjointed and incoherent, which can have the unintended effect of making a PRT's operations personality-driven.[45]

PRT command and control (C2) structures are not easily explained as each entity of the team, whether military or civilian, has a supervisor or commander in a separate chain of command. At each superior echelon in turn, this nexus extends upward into a quagmire of C2 where multiple lines of command and authority converge, making unity of command an impossibility and placing emphasis on the command element to corral unity of effort.[46] The quest for unity of effort is often complicated by separate, often opposing, objectives from multiples lines of authority. Further complicating this paradigm, coupled with the flexibility offered to PRTs to conduct missions in the OE, the convoluted C2 structure confuses many, "particularly in the NGO and international donor

---

[45] U.S. House of Representatives, *Agency Stovepipes vs Strategic Agility,* 20.

[46] USJFCOM, "Provincial Reconstruction Teams," 8.

community, about what a PRT is, what it ought to do, and what its limits should be."[47] In

an attempt to understand PRT C2 structures, the following pages first describe the

external C2 structures associated with PRTs and conclude with describing PRTs' internal

C2 structures.

As illustrated on the following page in Figure 8, C2 structures external to PRTs

include multiple agencies and command authorities.

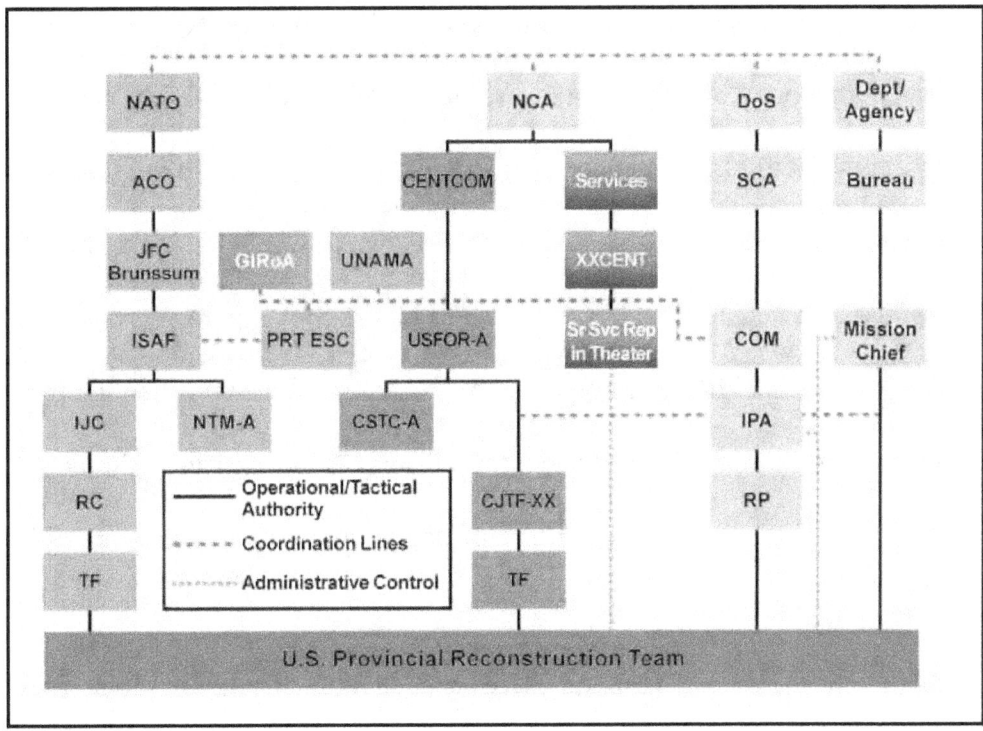

Figure 8: Lines of Authority.[48]

[47] U.S. Agency for International Development, "Provincial Reconstruction Teams in Afghanistan: An Interagency Assessment," (Washington DC: Government Printing Office, June 2006), 9.

[48] Center for Army Lessons Learned, *Afghanistan Provincial Reconstruction Team,* 32. Acronyms used: ACO – Allied Command Operations; CENTCOM – U.S. Central Command; CJTF – Combined Joint Task Force; CSTA-A – Combined Security Transition Command-Afghanistan; COM – Chief of Mission; DoS – Department of State; GIRoA – Government of the Islamic Republic of Afghanistan; IJC – ISAF Joint Command; ISAF – International Security Assistance Force; IPA – Interagency Provincial Affairs; JFC – Joint Force Command; NATO – North Atlantic Treaty Organization; NCA – National Command Authority; NTM-A – NATO Training Mission-Afghanistan; PRT ESC – PRT Executive Steering Committee; RC – Regional Command; RP – Regional Platform; SCA – Bureau of South and Central Asia; TF – Task Force; UNAMA – United National Assistance Mission in Afghanistan; USFOR-A – U.S. Forces-Afghanistan.

Figure 8 clearly outlines that the PRT is at the convergence of International Security Assistance Force (ISAF), United States Forces – Afghanistan (USFOR-A), Department of State, and other department/agency chains of command. What the C2 structure in Figure 8 does not accurately display is the number of other agencies which may be involved with PRTs, including USAID, U.S. Department of Agriculture, and U.S. Department of Justice, not to mention many local, national, and international agencies.

Focusing on the direction that is provided to PRTs in the execution of stability operations, another point of discussion is how national-level direction is translated into tactical action by PRTs. In Washington, direction for PRTs rests with the Policy Coordinating Committee of the National Security Council, where the policy travels through Ambassadorial and CENTCOM channels before trickling down to PRTs.[49] As depicted in Figure 8, the PRT Executive Steering Committee (ESC) is habitually linked with GIRoA ministerial-level and ISAF command-level leadership and is in the PRT's chain of command. However, the ESC lacks sufficient authority to guide the PRT efforts writ large.[50]

Operationally, U.S. PRTs are primarily guided by the Combined Joint Task Force (CJTF) Commander who is dual-hatted as the Regional Command (RC) Commander. This allows the CJTF Commander via the maneuver force commander to assign (or reassign) PRT efforts to other missions in the OE.[51] This arrangement brings into question the level of authority given to the PRT ESC and the alignment of the organization relative to the operational chain of command that is ultimately directing

---

[49] U.S. House of Representatives, "Agency Stovepipes vs Strategic Agility," 20

[50] Ibid., 21.

[51] Ibid., 20.

PRT operations. To further complicate the command and control picture, many task force commanders at the brigade combat team or regimental combat team level also "have their own governance, rule of law, and development programs that may complement, conflict, or duplicate the work of the PRTs."[52]

Within the PRT there are also challenges with command and control. Because of the civil-military structure of the PRT, the three principal agencies – Department of Defense, Department of State, and U.S. Agency for International development – form a triumvirate of command and control within the unit where each member reports through their own chain of command.[53]

From the outset, the DOD intended on the establishment and implementation of PRTs and PRT operations to span the CIV-MIL spectrum of U.S., Afghan, and international organizations. To enable this concept, the PRT's command structure includes a military commander, a Department of State Foreign Service Officer, a U.S. Agency for International Development Foreign Service Officer, and a U.S. Department of Agriculture representative.[54] In each PRT these individuals form the Integrated Command Group, which amounts to the command element that "is responsible for taking ISAF top-level direction and, in combination with U.S. national priorities, determining the PRT strategy to include approach, objectives, planned activities, and monitoring and evaluation systems."[55] The Integrated Command Group thus becomes a, if not the, critical component of the PRT; without a truly integrated command group, the PRT

---

[52] Ibid., 21.

[53] Ibid., 20.

[54] Center for Army Lessons Learned, *Afghanistan Provincial Reconstruction Team*, 41.

[55] Ibid., 43.

would not be able to combine and synchronize disparate objectives and lines of operation, much less conduct operations with unity of effort.[56] Yet while the military commander leads the command group as the senior partner, the command structure lacks coherence and relies "on getting the right personalities together at the right place and time."[57]

The PRT commander is either a U.S. Air Force lieutenant colonel or a U.S. Navy commander. Upon selection as a PRT commander, service members attend training including the Foreign Service Institute Reconstruction and Stabilization Course in Washington DC, a pre-deployment site survey to the Afghan province where they will be assigned, the ISAF COIN Academy in Kabul, Afghanistan-Pakistan Hands cultural training, staff training, combat skills training, and four months of language training.[58] PRT commander responsibilities include:[59]

- Commanding the military component of the PRT.
- Developing PRT strategies in conjunction with the integrated command group.
- Conducting key leader engagements with high-level GIRoA officials.
- Coordinating project funding with PRT elements.
- Ensuring all lines of authority have the same situational awareness on PRT activities/issues.
- Harmonizing all activities within the lines of operations and understanding the network of PRT tasks.

PRT civilian personnel experience a different set of pre-deployment training. Guided by the Special Representative for Afghanistan and Pakistan (SRAP) Interagency Training Working Group and implemented by Department of State's Foreign Service Institute, civilian team members receive a compliment of language, cultural, and combat

---

[56] Ibid.

[57] Ibid.

[58] U.S. Air Force Central Command, "Talking Paper on Provincial Reconstruction Team (PRT) Commander Selection Process," (AFCENT A1P: no date).

[59] Center for Army Lessons Learned, *Afghanistan Provincial Reconstruction Team,* 43.

skills training.[60] Pre-deployment training aims to gain an understanding of PRT roles

and responsibilities, develop PRT skill sets, build interagency PRT ties, gain an

understanding of the OE, and share lessons learned with current and previous PRT

officers.[61] Civilian team member responsibilities are listed below.

Department of State representative responsibilities include:[62]

- Developing PRT strategies in conjunction with the integrated command group.
- Being the lead on policy, governance, and political issues.
- Political reporting through various lines of authority.
- Conducting key leader engagements with local actors (e.g. governor, elders, and tribal leaders).

USAID and USDA representative responsibilities include:[63]

- Developing PRT strategies in conjunction with the integrated command group.
- Providing development advice to the PRT and local governance and agricultural structures.
- Performing PRT development interventions (projects, programs, and policy)
- Conducting key leader engagements with development actors (e.g. governor, donors, UN, and nongovernmental organizations).

Similar to how the PRT's mission and commander's intent focuses on the conduct

stability operations, its organizational structure is also decidedly so. The PRT's disparate

CIV-MIL organization enables the unit to conduct specialized missions in the OE. Even

though divergent guidance from multiple agencies guides PRTs, because they focus on

conducting stability operations (versus combat operations), PRTs are able to produce

effects in the OE within each of the five stability operations functions.

---

[60] J. Edward Fox, "Preparing Civilians for Deployment to Civilian-Military Platforms in Combat Environments," 51-2.

[61] USAID website, "Training for Provincial Reconstruction Teams," http://www.usaid.gov/our_work/global_partnerships/ma/prt.html, (accessed February 29, 2012).

[62] Center for Army Lessons Learned, *Afghanistan Provincial Reconstruction Team,* 44.

[63] Ibid.

While the PRT military and civilian members' responsibilities closely align and certainly nest with the PRT's mission and stability operations functions, the members' training is neither conducted together nor managed by a common organization. Part of this incongruence is because military personnel and civilian personnel deploy for different lengths of time (military members for nine months and civilian members for six months, one year, or longer, depending on the position) and their deployment dates are not aligned.

The effects of this circumstance are twofold. First, it negates the possibility to build a cohesive Integrated Command Group. Second, it negates the possibility for command and staff echelons above and adjacent to PRTs to understand PRT operations and build relationships with PRT Integrated Command Groups. In turn, this hampers higher and adjacent echelons' ability to nest PRT operations in the greater scheme of operations in the OE. While the problem of misaligned PRT leadership rotations is significant, it is but a symptom of a larger problem of a disjointed command and control structure.

The PRT's internal organization is decidedly focused to perform stability operations. The CIV-MIL mix of personnel, while heavily weighted to the military side, includes a healthy mix of administrative, support, and security personnel teamed with specialized skill sets that are unique to PRTs. It is this mixture of personnel and the resulting capabilities at the provincial level that extends the reach of higher-level, whole of government stability operations efforts to the provincial and district levels of government in Afghanistan.

Yet as the PRT is at the nexus of the U.S. Government's whole of government stability operations effort, it lacks several elements that would enhance its accomplishment of the stability operations mission. First, because it is an *ad hoc* unit, it cannot form habitual relationships, either within the unit, with adjacent units, or with superior organizations, until it is deployed into theater and conducting operations. Second, the mechanisms that select personnel for PRTs are disjointed, span multiple agencies, and do not take into account personalities inside or outside the team. This results in PRTs often "building the airplane while it's flying," where the unit is forming internal relationships, learning the mission, forming external relationships with Afghan officials, and forming external relationships with superior U.S. echelons while conducting operations. While this situation may be a necessary evil of any ad hoc organization, it does not need to be a *fait accompli*; it can be changed.

Thirdly, and linked to the previous point, the larger structure of PRT assignment, training, and implementation is as haphazard as PRT personnel assignment matters. As stated in a U.S. House of Representatives Committee on Armed Services report, "…while "personalities matter," the nation's security should not have to rely on having compatible personalities to successfully carry out the mission." Separate personnel, funding, and guidance agencies and directives negate any chance of unity of command within PRTs and make unity of effort a significant challenge. As was illustrated in Chapter 2, unity of command and clear policy direction was key to the execution of U.S. stability operations in post-war Japan; yet even with the benefit of hindsight, current PRT command and control structures are complicated and do not support unity of command or unity of effort. "Absent a comprehensive strategy from Washington or from CENTCOM headquarters, the directions of PRTs has been *ad hoc* and personality driven."[64]

The disjointed nature of PRTs' overarching command and control structures to establish, implement, guide, unify, and assess PRTs in Afghanistan is a significant point of discussion as it encumbers PRT operations within the greater war effort. However, it is also a point for additional consideration as it directly links to how PRTs use one of their primary weapon systems – money – and the funding streams associated therewith.

Finance

Funding is not consolidated for stability operations at the provincial and local levels and funding streams are extremely confusing.[65]

If the PRT's specialized personnel and staff sections are seen as the ways that the PRT conducts stability operations, the financial assets that the PRT uses are the associated means. PRTs in Afghanistan increase stability through improving the effectiveness of governance and the will of the people to be governed. To this end, PRTs employ funds in the form of "money as a weapon system" to build governance structures and popular support. PRTs utilize a range of engagement strategies to accomplish this, including supporting the government by building government facilitates and building popular support by building roads, bridges, and micro-hydro power facilities.[66]

PRTs primarily employ the Commander's Emergency Response Program (CERP) funding stream in conducting operations because the bureaucratic processes governing

---

[64] Ibid., 18.

[65] Ibid., 22.

[66] Michelle Parker, "Programming Development Funds to Support a Counterinsurgency: A Case Study of Nangahar, Afghanistan in 2006," (Center for Technology and National Security Policy), 6.

CERP are relatively streamlined within military organizations.[67] CERP aims to provide Commanders with a quick, effective, non-kinetic method to achieve immediate impact to the Afghan population.[68]

U.S. Forces Afghanistan (USFOR-A) Publication 1-06, *Money as a Weapons System Afghanistan* (MAAWS-A) details the MAAWS-A program and its implementation. CERP is a program that Commanders use "to respond to urgent **humanitarian relief** and **reconstruction** requirements in their Area of Responsibility (AOR) by carrying out programs that will immediately assist the indigenous population."[69] (Emphasis in original.) CERP projects are intended to be sustained by Afghans, to provide employment for Afghans, and "to build capacity, promote peace and hope for future generations, and build trust and lasting support for the GIRoA."[70] Commanders can use CERP in many ways, ranging from agriculture, education, and electricity projects to Rule of Law & Governance improvements.

CERP authorities range from the USCENTCOM Commander, who oversees the use of the program in the USCENTCOM AOR and advocates for resources and authorities to support the program, to U.S. Field Commanders who identify, approve, and manage CERP projects within their AOR.[71] Commanders are responsible for ensuring that "CERP funds achieve maximum results, which includes establishing performance

---

[67] Ibid.

[68] U.S. Forces Afghanistan, *Money As A Weapon System,* 11.

[69] Ibid., 10.

[70] Ibid., 10-11.

[71] Ibid., 19.

objectives and monitoring progress," as well as developing and implementing processes for focusing the effects of CERP within their AOR.[72]

While CERP affords field Commanders great flexibility to conduct stability operations in Afghanistan by supporting counterinsurgency objectives, the program's effectiveness remains largely unknown. The Special Inspector General for Afghanistan Reconstruction (SIGAR) recently completed a study of CERP projects in Laghman Province spanning fiscal years 2008-2010, totaling $53.3 million of obligated funds.[73] Although USFOR-A Pub 1-06 states that CERP is for "urgent humanitarian needs and COIN objectives,"[74] SIGAR found that 92 percent of the inspected projects were "at risk for questionable outcomes" and generally addressed medium and long-term needs.[75] Construction of asphalt roads and new buildings were cited as primary concerns due to lack of Afghan capacity and/or capability to maintain the completed projects.[76]

Additionally, although SIGAR'S "analysis did not take into account other factors that may determine a successful counterinsurgency outcome, such as the perceived legitimacy of government of Afghanistan, measures of corruption, differences in economic growth, or the number of insurgent attacks,"[77] it cited that USFOR-A "lacks a coordinated, results-oriented approach for evaluating the effectiveness of CERP

---

[72] Ibid., 31.

[73] Office of the Special Inspector General for Afghanistan Reconstruction, "Commander's Emergency Response Program in Laghman Province Provided Some Benefits, but Oversight Weaknesses and Sustainment Concerns Led to Questionable Outcomes and Potential Waste," (Washington, D.C.: January 27, 2011), 1.

[74] U.S. Forces Afghanistan, *Money As A Weapon System,* 11.

[75] Office of the Special Inspector General for Afghanistan Reconstruction, "Commander's Emergency Response Program in Laghman Province," 5.

[76] Ibid., 6.

[77] Ibid.,

projects"[78] and that field units "did not have formal mechanisms in place to track and assess project outcomes" and "relied on anecdotal information from villagers to report problems with completed projects."[79]

PRT Laghman Summary

The preceding analysis of PRT Laghman gives the reader an understanding of how PRT operations in Afghanistan link with overall stability operations and the greater war efforts undertaken by ISAF and USFOR-A. PRTs absolutely have a positive effect; however, many limitations still exist within the current PRT construct that hamper overall effectiveness. These limitations and recommendations for their mitigation are discussed in the following chapter.

---

[78] Ibid., 17.

[79] Ibid., 18.

CHAPTER 4: RECOMMENDATIONS AND CONCLUSION

There is little doubt that since the 9/11 terrorist attacks on the United States, the U.S. military has accomplished a significant shift toward organizing, training, and equipping to conduct counterinsurgency and stability operations. The impending financial reductions that the U.S. military is facing will force the DOD to make difficult decisions on what capabilities to keep at full strength, which ones to keep at reduced capacity, and which ones to shelf altogether.

Seemingly caught in the middle of this argument are stability operations-focused forces. As current DOD direction focuses upon military core competencies as they would be employed in the Asia-Pacific region, stability operations force structure will almost inevitably be reduced.[1] Yet as these decisions fall upon the DOD and it postures U.S. military forces for the next conflict, over ten years of stability operations expertise is at risk of being lost as stability operations forces remain uncodified within the U.S. military's force structure. Without codification in practice – meaning that specific units are organized, trained, and equipped for the conduct of stability operations – the lessons and expertise from the wars in Iraq and Afghanistan will likely fall into the annals of history only to be relearned in future wars.

The PRT is a key asset in the conduct of stability operations as it combines specialized capabilities in a CIV-MIL structure capable of operating in semi-permissive environments. This construct provides the DOD with unique stability operations

---

[1] U.S. Department of Defense, *Sustaining U.S. Global Leadership: Priorities for 21st Century Defense*, (January 2012), 6.

capabilities and a unit that is able to produce effects within each of the five stability operations functions.

Yet even as PRTs' contributions have been noted and the DOD has issued guidance in DODI 3000.05 directing the services to organize, train, and equip for stability operations,[2] the U.S. military has not codified the PRT model; PRTs remain in existence only as *ad hoc* units. In order to institutionally codify the stability operations lessons from the wars in Iraq and Afghanistan and to ensure that Combatant Commanders are armed with adequate stability operations capabilities for future conflicts, the PRT or a variant thereof must become a standing unit within the United States military.

The institutionalization of PRTs within the U.S. military would ensure the codification of stability operations of the current conflicts as well as for future stability operations. It would also facilitate habitual command relationships – both military and civilian – within command structures, which would educate echelons above and adjacent to PRTs as to the conduct of stability operations and what tools the PRTs bring in executing operations within the stability functions.

Sufficient guidance and doctrine exists at the DOD and Joint Force levels to guide the codification of the PRT or a PRT-like unit in the U.S. military. What remains opaque is the intent behind the guidance provided by DODI 3000.05 and JP 3-07. The evolution of both documents is very recent and certainly directly linked to the wars in Iraq and Afghanistan. This begs the question as to whether the DOD has developed this guidance and doctrine to guide the Joint Force in the future or merely to justify the breadth and depth of current stability operations. This notion is further underscored by the lack of an

---

[2] U.S. Department of Defense, *DOD Instruction 3000.05: Stability Operations*, (September 16, 2009), 13.

executive agent (military service) to "own" the DOTMLPF implications of a standing stability operations force; without such ownership, the future of just such a codified force is unlikely.

Another key hurdle in the institutionalization of PRTs is codifying the civilian-military aspect of the PRT. In order to achieve this, interagency coordination must centralize and streamline funding, personnel, and authority issues for the PRT to reach its full potential. As such, the DOD must coordinate with other departments of the U.S. government and enact significant changes to current force structures. These force structure changes would also extend into theater operations, streamlining command and control structures to where the nexus of CIV-MIL integration occurs at a theater command level rather than at the tactical unit level.

Provided that this change occurs, the entire calculus of the PRT could correspondingly change. Assuming that the theater headquarters effectively meshes a whole of government approach to stability operations, the PRT mission could become a military-only mission. In other words, rather than the PRT remaining the nexus of a whole-of-government approach thereby demanding a CIV-MIL structure, the whole-of-government approach would be enacted at a theater command level and executed by a military-only PRT. In such a case the military-only PRT would provide whole-of-government effects in the OE as enabled by whole-of-government integration at the theater level.

Although the model presented by U.S. PRTs in Afghanistan has shortcomings and would benefit from modifications, it provides a viable model for a unit focused on the conduct of stability operations.

BIBLIOGRAPHY

Ball, W. Macmahon. *Japan: Enemy or Ally?* New York: John Day, 1949.

Boot, Max. *The Savage Wars of Peace: Small Wars and the Rise of American Power*. New York: Basic Books, 2002.

Birtle, Andrew J. U.S. *Army Counterinsurgency and Contingency Operations Doctrine 1860-1941*. Washington DC: U.S. Government Printing Office, 1997.

Center for Army Lessons Learned. *Afghanistan Provincial Reconstruction Team: Observations, Insights, and Lessons*. February, 2011.

CJTF-101. "RC(E) Mission Briefing." Bagram Airfield, Afghanistan: November 5, 2010.

Crane, Staff Sergeant Ryan. "PRT Laghman Visits Local Hospital." August 24, 2011. http://www.dvidshub.net/image/447204/prt-laghman-visits-local-hospital#.T0k6sJjPVUQ (accessed February 25, 2012).

Dower, John W. *Embracing Defeat: Japan in the Wake of World War II*. New York: W.W. Norton & Company, 2000.

Fox, J. Edward. "Preparing Civilians for Deployment to Civilian-Military Platforms in Combat Environments: The Evolution fo Staffing and Training for the Civilian Mission in Afghanistan. in *Towards a Comprehensive Approach: Strategic and Operational Challenges*. Rome: NATO Defense College, May 2011.

Government of the Islamic Republic of Afghanistan. Ministry of Rural Rehabilitation and Development. http://mrrd.gov/af/en/page/67 (accessed September 29, 2011).

International Security Assistance Force website. http://www.nato.int/isaf/topics/prt/ (accessed October 22, 2011).

Japan Government. "Potsdam Declaration." National Diet Library. http://www.ndl.go.jp/constitution/e/etc/c06.html, (accessed January 4, 2012).

Major General Kasdorf. International Security Assistance Force teleconference. http://www.nato.int/isaf/docu/speech/2007/sp071011a.html, (accessed February 25, 2012).

Kamiya, Major General Jason K. Preface to *Provincial Reconctruction Teams.* Pre-doctrinal Research White Paper No. 07-01. Suffolk, VA: U.S. Joint Forces Command, November 21, 2007.

Linn, Brian McCallister. *The Philippine War, 1899-1902.* Lawrence, KS: University Press of Kansas, 2000.

Office of the Special Inspector General for Afghanistan Reconstruction. "Commander's Emergency Response Program in Laghman Province Provided Some Benefits, but Oversight Weaknesses and Sustainment Concerns Led to Questionable Outomces and Potential Waste." Washington DC, January 27, 2011.

Parker, Michelle. "Programming Development Funds to Support a Counterinsurgency: A Case Study of Nangahar, Afghanistan in 2006." Washington DC: Center for Technology and National Security Policy.

PRT Laghman. "PRT Laghman Command Briefing." FOB Mehtar Lam, Afghanistan: November 5, 2010.

Program of Culture and Conflict Studies. "Laghman Province." http://www.nps.edu/programs/ccs/Docs/Executive%20Summaries/Laghman_Provincial_Overview_CCS.pdf (accessed February 25, 2012).

RC-East website. http://www.isaf.nato.int/subordinate-commands/rc-east/index.php (accessed February 25, 2012).

Rogers, Catherine. "The Interagency Process in Reconstruction of Post-World War II Japan." in *Stability Operations and State Building*, 171-207. Carlisle, PA: Strategic Studies Insititute, 2008. http://www.isn.ethz.ch/isn/Digital-library/Publications/Detail/?ots591=cab359a3-9328-19cc-ald2-8023e646b22c&lng=en&id=48234 (accessed January 4, 2012).

Schaefer, Peter F. and P. Clayton Schaefer. "Planning for Reconstruction and Transformation of Japan after World War II." in *Stability Operations and State Building*, 171-207. Carlisle, PA: Strategic Studies Insititute, 2008. http://www.isn.ethz.ch/isn/Digital-library/Publications/Detail/?ots591=cab359a3-9328-19cc-ald2-8023e646b22c&lng=en&id=92327 (accessed January 4, 2012).

Stimson, Henry L. and McGeorge Bundy. *On Active Service in Peace and War.* New York: Harper & Brothers, 1947.

U.S. Agency for International Development. "Provincial Reconstruction Teams in Afghanistan: An Interagency Assessment." Washington DC: Government Printing Office, June 2006.

U.S. Agency for International Development website. "Training for Provincial Reconstruction Teams." http://www.usaid.gov/our_work/global_partnerships/ma/prt.html, (accessed February 29, 2012).

U.S. Department of Defense. *DoD Directive 3000.05: Stability Operations.* Washington DC: Department of Defense, November 2005.

_____. *DoD Instruction 3000.05: Stability Operations.* Washington DC: Department of Defense, September 2009.

_____. *Sustaining U.S. Global Leadership: Priorities for 21st Century Defense.* Washington DC: Government Printing Office, January 2012.

U.S. Forces Afghanistan. *Money As A Weapon System (MAAWS-A).* USFOR-A Pub 1-06. Commander's Emergency Respons Program (CERP) SOP. Kabul, Afghanistan. http://www.michaelyon-online.com/images/pdf/maaws-feb-2011-1.pdf (accessed February 25, 2012).

U.S. House of Representatives. Committee on Armed Services. Subcommittee on Oversight & Investigations. *Agency Stovepipes vs Strategic Agility: Lessons We Need to Learn from Provincial Reconstruction Teams in Iraq and Afghanistan.* Washington DC: Government Printing Office, April 2008.

U.S. Joint Chiefs of Staff. *Department of Defense Dictionary of Military and Associated Terms.* Joint Publication 1-02. Washington DC: Joint Chiefs of Staff, May 15, 2011.

_____. *Joint Operation Planning.* Joint Publication 5-0. Washington DC: Joint Chiefs of Staff, August 11, 2011.

_____. *Stability Operations.* Joint Publication 3-07. Washington DC: Joint Chiefs of Staff, September 29, 2011.

Vincelli, Captain Tony. "Provincial Reconstruction Team Uses Infantry Soldiers to Bolster Joint Patrols." Laghman Province, Afghanistan: September 1, 2011. http://www.centcom.mil/news/provincial-reconstruction-team-uses-infantry-soldiers-to-bolster-joint-patrols (accessed February 25, 2012).

Weckerlein, Staff Sergeant Julie. "Afghans Train Afghans with American Mentorship." Laghman Province, Afghanistan: September 11, 2007. http://www.af.mil/news/story.asp?id-123067439 (accessed February 25, 2012).